11th Hour Preparedness

Making Choices While We Can

Tyler Woods

authorHOUSE

AuthorHouse™
1663 Liberty Drive
Bloomington, IN 47403
www.authorhouse.com
Phone: 1-800-839-8640

© 2010 Tyler Woods. All rights reserved.

No part of this book may be reproduced, stored in a retrieval system, or transmitted by any means without the written permission of the author.

First published by AuthorHouse   8/31/2010

ISBN: 978-1-4520-6289-1 (e)
ISBN: 978-1-4520-6287-7 (sc)

Library of Congress Control Number: 2010912894

Printed in the United States of America
Bloomington, Indiana

This book is printed on acid-free paper.

Foreword

Foreword by:
Michael J. Arnold
President and Lead Instructor
Staying Alive, Inc.

I was once asked, "Let me get this straight. You make a living teaching people how to kill each other?"

After considering the probable intelligence level of the questioner, I thought it best to keep the answer as simple as possible; "Absolutely not—I teach people, who find themselves in very bad situations, how to win and then go home alive." I teach my students that the manner in which they handle the first 10 seconds of a serious social encounter will most likely determine who goes home alive.

Tyler Woods has taken my job to the next level. While my instruction concentrates on the first 10 yards of the 100 yard dash, **11th Hour Preparedness** is the instruction manual for winning a marathon. It's for the folks who have come home, and found that home is not as they left it.

11th Hour Preparedness is a no nonsense guide for those who find that they have to become their own farmers, grocers, doctors, firemen and policemen.

Foreword by Tyler Woods, author

For the most part, when we are faced with conflicting messages and uncertain times, our tendency is to continue life as we know it and wait for the confusion to pass. That could prove a drastic mistake in today's economy. First we were told that the country was experiencing an economic downturn. As unemployment became commonplace and home values dropped, we were told that we are in a recession. Now our government analysts and financial experts are freely using the ugly term, depression. The problem is that the depression our grandparents experienced caused many to follow their employment from the northern states to southern states where pay was less but the cost of living provided a livable situation. Demand for honest labor continued through those rough years and we came out of it. That scenario doesn't fit today's situation. Hundreds of thousands of unemployed are willing to work but unable to support their families with available jobs. For countless workers, they can't relocate to resume jobs that have moved to India, Mexico or Asia. If they could move, they can't sell their house for what they still owe on the mortgage. Depression is ugly and projections for this one are long, deep and slow.

We have become dependent on an infrastructure of services. Water comes from the tap, heat and air-conditioning from vents in the floor and communication is as close as the nearest cell tower. Every aspect of our lives has become dependent on a web of interrelated services. We have been led to believe that our services are robust with prolonged outages all but non-existent. Truth is a casualty to advertisement and current events show cracks in our system of service and supply. The recent heat wave on the east coast of America is bringing concern of a regional failure of the electric grid. Financial ruin, brought about by outsourcing industry to offshore countries, has left Detroit and Lansing Michigan to the place where without federal aid, they can't continue city services. Adverse weather causes a run on grocery stores and gas stations leaving empty shelves in the first twenty-four hours and empty service stations after two days.

What if an event or series of events caused a total collapse of our services? Financial default at the federal level; population loss due to a medical pandemic; terrorist acts on a grand scale; dirty bomb; EMP device; nuclear attack... the list goes on with each growing more possible every day. How would we live if our services were suddenly stopped? Do we have what it takes to live without grocery stores, the internet, running water and electricity? The pages that follow will help you assess your environment against liabilities, develop a plan to improve your situation and equip yourself with skills and supplies to better your chances in desperate times. Today, food and supply is affordable, resources are available and options are abundant. This may not remain true in the future, but for those who prepare themselves and their families to live less dependent on systems and services, they will become new pioneers.

Tyler

Acknowledgments:

What started as a few notes for a seminar on the subject of "current needs for preparedness," grew to become **11th Hour Preparedness**. The effort to reclaim our independence from the systems of easy living, has jumped to a new level in the past few years. Evidence now indicates that we have less time to prepare than was previously thought. As the data came together, it became more apparent how necessary this book is for us today.

My thanks has to go first, to the originators of self-reliance, our pioneering ancestors. Our grandparents and great grandparents cut wagon trails, built railroads, chiseled highways through mountains and raised families without the assistance of electricity, telephones, grocery stores and the internet.

Thanks needs to be made to the many authors of great preparedness books and manuals that have become the foundation of what we update today. I couldn't imagine the effort necessary to create all that data from scratch.

The support of my wife and family has been without question, instrumental in helping me as they patiently put up with the loss of my time and attention and endured countless readings and remarks of "how's this sound?" Thank you from the bottom of my heart! It is with my deepest gratitude that I dedicate this book to Terry, my best friend and wife of 33 years.

Tyler Woods

Finally, I thank my friends and editors who assisted in the cleaning up of rough manuscript. Mike and Pat Arnold, of Staying Alive Inc., gave their time and knowledge to validating the subject matter and grammatical editing while Jason Bond assisted with grammatical editing and orderly flow of the completed material. This book reflects your hard work and my thanks.

Contents

Foreword	v
Acknowledgments:	ix
Are we there yet?	1
What It Takes to Survive:	7
THE SYSTEM:	11
START A NOTEBOOK:	15
One Mogul at a Time	21
Where to Start:	25
Begin at Home:	41
FUEL:	61
First-Aid:	67
Firearms:	71
BEYOND THE FIRST FOUR:	83
FAITH: the Fifth "F"	105
The Why of What We Do:	109
COMING OUT:	113
THE NEXT STEP:	117

11th HR

Are we there yet?

Preparedness guidelines that have remained unchanged for decades are now obsolete. Those who fail to change with the new paradigm will find their resources grossly inadequate to meet the needs of a drastically altered game plan. The world is a different place than it was 30 years ago. Current scenarios that remove our support infrastructure, for much longer than previously anticipated, are now more likely than ever. Today, even veterans of preparedness are finding themselves students again. We all have a lot of work to do.

Is America on the brink of disaster? Could we wake up one day to find our world suddenly and dramatically changed? Many knowledgeable authorities think so. Watch the news stories, both domestic and foreign, regarding American business, unemployment, health, government and threats that might affect the quality of life we have grown to expect in this country. They point to a universal belief that

America is not healthy and is headed for serious trouble. Here are some of those headlines:

Telegraph.UK By Ambrose Evans-Pritchard Published: 6:35PM GMT 10 Jan 2010
America slides deeper into depression as Wall Street revels
December was the worst month for US unemployment since the Great Recession began.

Thomas Ferraro WASHINGTON Tue Dec 22, 2009 6:19pm EST
Senate sets Christmas eve vote on U.S. debt limit
WASHINGTON (Reuters) - The U.S. Senate on Tuesday set a Christmas Eve vote on final congressional approval of a bill to provide a two-month increase in the federal debt limit.

Updated January 20, 2010AP
Senate Democrats Propose $1.9T Increase to U.S. Debt Limit
WASHINGTON -- Senate Democrats on Wednesday proposed allowing the federal government to borrow an additional $1.9 trillion to pay its bills, a record increase that would permit the national debt to reach $14.3 trillion.

Breaking from Moneynews.com
Foreigners Dropping Treasury Securities at Record Rate
A record drop in foreign holdings of U.S. Treasury bills in December sent a reminder that the government might have to pay higher interest rates on its debt to continue to attract investors.

Thursday, 18 Feb 2010 | 8:39 AM ET By: Reuters
Jobless Claims, Inflation Jump as Economy Wobbles
The number of U.S. workers filing new applications for unemployment insurance unexpectedly surged last week, while producer prices increased sharply in January, raising potential hurdles for the economic recovery.

Updated December 24, 2009 AP

Senate Votes to Raise Debt Ceiling to $12.4 Trillion
The Senate's rare Christmas Eve vote allows the Treasury Department to issue enough bonds to fund the government's operations and programs until mid-February.

Published: January 20 2010 16:46 | Last updated: January 20 2010 16:46 By Peter Garnham
Russia diversifies into Canadian dollars (and away from US dollars)
Russia's central bank announced on Wednesday that it had started buying Canadian dollars and securities in a bid to diversify its foreign exchange reserves. (They are diversifying away from US currency)

FOXNews.com
Obama Shatters Spending Record for First-Year Presidents
The federal government spent $3.5 trillion during President Obama's first year in office. This far exceeds the spending for any other first-year president.

The New York Times | 23 Nov 2009 | 06:29 AM ET
Wave of Debt Payments Facing US Government
The United States government is financing its more than trillion-dollar-a-year borrowing with i.o.u.'s on terms that seem too good to be true. But that happy situation, aided by ultralow interest rates, may not last much longer.

AP
Unemployment Report Expected to Be Grim
When the Labor Department releases the January unemployment report Friday, it will also update its estimate of jobs lost in the year that ended in March 2009. The number is expected to rise by roughly 800,000, raising the number of jobs shed during the recession to around 8 million.

Thursday, December 03, 2009
Maryland Reports First Drug Resistant H1N1 Cases
BALTIMORE — Maryland health officials are reporting the state's first two known cases of swine flu resistant to Tamiflu.

Below is a chart showing the recent growth in the number of unemployed people who have not found work after six months of searching. These have exhausted their unemployment resources. News stories listing a decrease in claims for unemployment will show this data in a positive light but keep in mind, the people represented by this chart are still unemployed and they have exhausted their eligibility to make further claims.

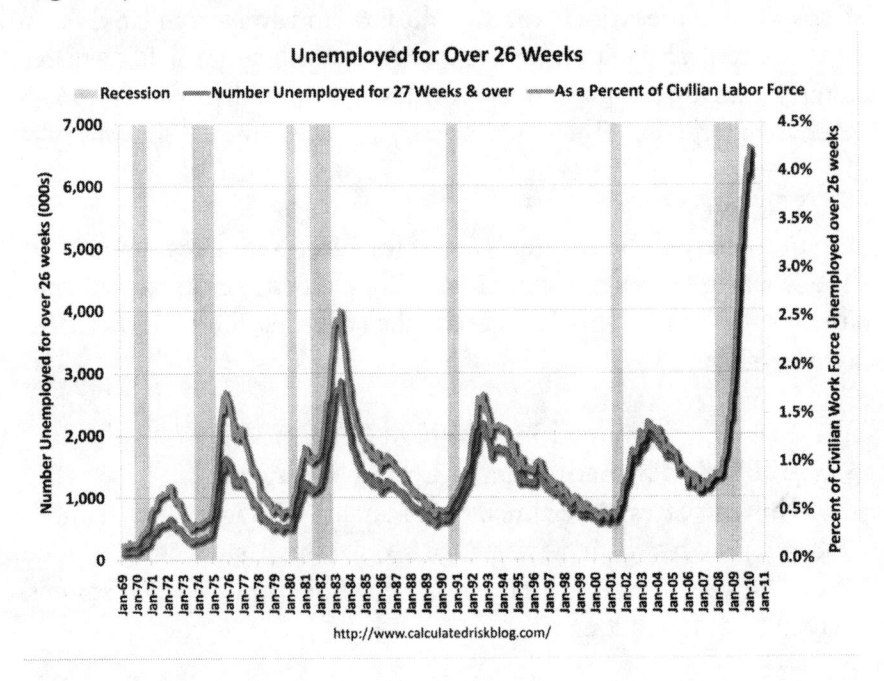

Unemployed for Over 26 Weeks

Chart source: http://www.calculatedriskblog.com/

There are many more articles and data supporting these alarming facts. I stopped collecting because supporting articles are in the paper every day. Nearly 5% of our civilian workforce has been unemployed for over twenty-six weeks. Were it not for federal extensions, our front page headlines would read like those of the great depression. The same articles that hail the end of recession, include comments that unemployment and home foreclosures may continue to increase. Who is the media trying to kid?

If there was ever an opportune time for adversity, America is in it. Our economy is on the verge of collapse from the weight of its own debt. Terrorists are actively planning attacks on American soil. We are ripe for a medically resistant epidemic. Acts of nature can shut down regions of our country for long periods of time and if that's not enough, any one of us could lose our job and face extended unemployment.

Fox News recently reported that 79% of Americans believe our country is headed for economic failure and that our government officials do not have remedy to avoid it. International experts have been saying this for years. We aren't so powerful that it can't happen to us. It happened to the USSR and they charted for us what we could expect. Overnight their money became worthless and the only thing of value was food and water. It took the emerging nine Baltic States an average of six months to develop a temporary script to serve as money. Real money, that could be exchanged for other currency of the world, took five years to be established.

Terrorism in our own country is now routine. Attempts to create mass carnage are being discovered in advanced planning stages. Many of us wonder when the next attempt will be successful.

The Pacific Northwest is expecting a massive earthquake from the two geological plates beneath them. These tectonic plates have been jammed for decades and building energy as they literally elevate a mountain range. When it lets go, there aren't many buildings expected to remain standing.

Blizzards on the east coast recently demonstrated that we can't depend on our local grocery store for food supply. Ahead of almost any storm, grocery shelves are stripped clean, gas stations are pumped dry and those who don't prepare early are just out of luck. You might be inconvenienced if you had to rely on food in your pantry for a few days but in the face of prolonged failure of the system, it could grow much more serious.

If you are not fully convinced that at least one of these threats are real and likely to happen, the rest of this book may not be for you. For those who see the danger and wish to prepare their family to refuse to become victims, this book is for you.

11th HR

What It Takes to Survive:

The elite unit of the British army, called the Special Air Service (SAS), teaches their men that the ability to survive is based on three elements. Those elements are displayed in a pyramid divided into three layers. The foundation, and most important layer, is the **"Will to Survive."**

I was in the USAF during Vietnam and our training covered aspects of survival. I learned a story demonstrating the importance of the will to live that stuck with me. An American pilot had to ditch his plane deep into a desert when his fighter jet flamed out. His radio had failed and no one knew where he went down. Search was without success and the pilot was given up for dead. The pilot, on the other hand, was not so inclined to give up on himself. Knowing that his location was unknown to his searchers, he began walking out in the direction he knew lead to his base. After three days of walking without water, the pilot was found. He had several cuts and superficial wounds that did not bleed until he was given water. His blood was too thick for his wounds to bleed! There was no explanation for how that pilot lived except for his determination not to die. The will to live can be the single most powerful element to survival.

The second layer of the pyramid is labeled **"Knowledge."** Knowledge instills confidence and dispels fear. I was given our family station wagon when I was in high school. It was a good car but the engine had a lot of miles on it and was tired. I set out to rebuild the engine. I had never rebuilt an engine before but I had a basic understanding of how engines worked and the auto parts store guided me in the necessary tasks. In a few weeks the engine was rebuilt and running. Someone asked me how I found the confidence to tackle such a project. My answer was that I never thought of it as something I shouldn't be able to do. I wonder how many have failed to begin projects because they lacked confidence, even though they had basic knowledge and the tools required?

The final layer of the pyramid is labeled **"Training."** Training is the exercise of skills to reach mastery then maintaining those skills in readiness. I have watched martial artists perform mock combat and it looks like a blur of hands and feet. I've often wondered how they blend so many complicated moves into blinding fast and fluid motion. Another mystery for me is to watch a pianist play a fast and complex movement. How do they get their fingers to move so quickly with each hand working independently? The answer to both questions is the same. The martial artist's actions, as well as the pianist's, are practiced slowly and deliberately, with attention to proper form and execution. As the routines are learned, the artist gains speed and fluid motion. Their body learns the moves in what is called muscle memory. This allows them to execute complex actions very quickly without having to think about each movement. Practice, drill and repetition will allow you to do the right thing almost automatically. It's called **"Training."**

If we were to put a cap on our pyramid, it would be labeled **"Survival Kit."** A basic survival kit would contain tools to use in applying our <u>will to live</u>, <u>knowledge</u> and <u>training</u>. That kit is your bug out backpack and should contain essential tools to allow you to survive: food, water, clothing, knife, rope, shelter, fire making devices and first aid. Your kit should grow as you learn more survival skills and acquire training to use them.

11th HR

THE SYSTEM:

"THE SYSTEM" refers to our current infrastructure of information and supply. Information is supplied by phone, television, radio and the internet. Food is supplied by local grocery stores. Power is distributed from a massive system called an electric grid. Fresh water is piped to our homes and sewage is piped away. Even our garbage is picked up regularly. Most system failures last only days to perhaps a few weeks but let me assure you, there are scenarios present which would take down THE SYSTEM for a long time and require at least six to twelve month's food supply for families who will be completely on their own. The six month supply applies only to those situations where the infrastructure can be restored. For those conditions where the systems cannot be regained (and there are many) a full twelve to eighteen month supply is necessary to sustain life until resources from your own garden, hunting and fishing become sufficient to supply all food requirements.

How fragile is THE SYSTEM? Take a close look at your grocery store. Massive amounts of almost any kind of food ever needed, right? Where did it all come from? Few items in our stores come from less than hundreds of miles away, some from much further. Even fresh bread, though baked locally, requires basic ingredients that are shipped in. Everything comes by truck. Since the efficiency movement found ways to avoid tax on inventoried products, stores don't "store" things like they used to. Computerized checkouts scan items and build inventory orders to THE SYSTEM for re-stock. National food warehouses (less than a dozen across the country) put together a distribution system that assures you will find cans of peas and corn on the shelf at all times, "just in time".... unless... something 'out of the ordinary' happens.

Napoleon learned what every military commander now knows. Long supply lines are fragile, can be easily disrupted and "the lack of supply" will defeat an army faster than any other enemy. Fragile supply lines that can't respond to sudden changes in demand are why store shelves empty in the path of storms and why gasoline is unavailable when masses of people try to leave town at the same time. Power grids depend on large numbers of workers to keep them operating, as do our water and sewer systems. Anything that disrupts these fragile systems will bring them down and leave stranded those who depend on them.

Domestic terrorism only has to disrupt our supply for little more than two weeks before anarchy tears society apart from the inside. Almost any major event can trigger street violence, smash-and-grab looting and social mayhem. Our police and National Guard are not sufficiently manned to address lawlessness on a grand scale. If one city gets out of hand, neighboring cities lend police resources to assist. When a larger area needs assistance the National Guard is called. Where would the resources come from if every city needed assistance? We don't have the resources to restore law and order on that grand scale. As stated in "The History Chanel" docu-drama After Armageddon "America is only about nine meals from anarchy."

http://www.youtube.com/watch?v=UlcYpgfI564 (Part 1 of 9)

None of the pieces of the system can stand independently. Everything depends on electricity, fuel, the internet, computing and armies of people to keep them running. If one piece of the system goes down it can take the entire house of cards with it.

I'm not saying anything new. There are many good books that document the frailty of our society. So why did I write this book? Why should you listen to me? Even better, why should you spend money to attend one of my seminars? Just one reason. I can help you become better prepared. By all indication, there may not be much time and preparation needs to start now. If money is no concern, various survival product websites enable credit card holders to spend their way to preparedness. If you are like the rest of us, you can use good advice from those with experience to help in making the best of limited resources. Preparedness doesn't have to empty a retirement account. Preparedness also includes more than can be purchased with a credit card.

My Credentials:

First of all, I refuse to become a victim. I've breezed through storms, hurricanes and a super-class typhoon. I've wobbled through earthquakes, waded through floods and shoveled through blizzards. In each of these declared "disasters", I was there to rescue the stranded, provide warmth and comfort to victims because I already had the required resources. My children recall those times as "camping in our living room." I come from a long line of self sufficient ancestors who would not let themselves get too dependent on the "comforts" of easy living. I don't mind being called "cheap." It's common sense to me. I've cut and split firewood to reduce energy costs to our budget, designed our home to use multiple energy sources, planted gardens, ground our flour, baked our bread and raised chickens. Now I watch my children do some of the same tasks for their families.

Second, I've discovered a lot of 'less than perfect' decisions that seemed good at fist. There are many apparently good ideas that can waste time and money. When time or money is limited, wasting it can cost in more ways than the obvious. My sister has a plaque that reads: "Learn from the mistakes of others, you don't have time to make all those mistakes yourself." I will share with you some of the popular thinking that leads astray and wastes resources.

Third, I've been studying and practicing preparedness for over thirty-five years, both civilian and military. During more than seventeen years with a major corporation in the Pacific Northwest, I became an area Safety Focal. I was responsible for organizing evacuation plans for large buildings and giving preparedness presentations at work, public high schools, county libraries and civic centers. Most general public audiences were sparsely attended except one. I was speaking at a public library in North Bend, WA. The day before my presentation, an earth tremor of about three point something shook the region. There weren't enough chairs for the crowd that evening.

Regrettably, the people who packed in to hear my presentation that night, probably went home and did nothing about it. A problem with preparedness is that it has to be done while things are calm and times are good. I'd guess even Joseph of Egypt had a difficult time collecting one fifth of the harvest to lay in store for the famine that had not yet come. The Biblical story of Joseph and the famine is appropriate here. If we do nothing until trouble starts, it will be too late to prepare. It does no good to agree with the need to prepare if you do nothing to make preparation. This is one reason I charge a fee to attend my seminars. Most people will do little with something easily gotten. The other reason I charge a fee is that I've invested countless hours preparing the material and have grown accustomed to eating warm food and sleeping indoors.

It is important that we start practicing the skills we acquire. I've learned that successful gardening does not come from book knowledge. It requires sweat, dirt and experience. The same is true for hunting, fishing, cooking, bread making and just about every task we need to learn. Whatever the task, if you think you can... try it. You'll be surprised at how many details you need to refine to become proficient.

11th HR

START A NOTEBOOK:

Preparing for an extended period of life without services is frustrated by the fact that we've become so dependent and comfortable letting others do our work for us. We expect the lights to turn on with the flip of a switch, water to flow by the turn of a handle, heat/AC to emerge because a thermostat was set and the garbage to disappear because we set the can on the curb. Laundry is cleaned by putting dirty clothes in a machine, adding a little detergent, turning the machine on and coming back later. When we come back, the wash is ready for the dryer. We live in a push-button world, and we like it. What happens when it all stops? When the power no longer comes to your house, the water no longer flows and the heat/AC won't come out of those floor vents? How will you get on with life?

What is your plan?

A preparedness plan will depend on location. If a home is in or very near a major metropolitan area, remaining there would be a mistake and by the time it is realized, it may be too late to correct it.

Evaluate your current home for several things. Can you continue living there without utilities? If the sewer system depends on electricity (all municipal systems are energy dependent) it will fail and may back up into the house. If you do not have a natural water source (well, spring or fresh water stream) it will fail after the power grid goes down. It all comes down to this: the city will be no place to live after these systems fail. Large numbers of city dwellers will realize this, creating a mass exodus within a few weeks of an outage. Gridlock will cause chaos on major roadways leading out of the city and fuel supplies will be exhausted. With removal of social controls (police/national guard) criminal elements will be unbridled. Looting and highway holdups will make travel extremely dangerous.

If you live in a major city, preparation needs to center on locating a safe place to go, stocking supplies at that location and keeping pre-packed "Bug-Out Bags" with enough food, water and essentials to get to that place. Prepare easily carried containers that can be quickly loaded into your vehicle and don't forget more than enough fuel to get there. Among the Bug-Out Bags should be fully contained backpacks for each person. It may become necessary to abandon the vehicles and continue on foot. Part of that plan needs to establish exactly what will trigger the decision to Bug-out. Denial will be your worst enemy. To linger in false hope of everything returning to normal could be a fatal mistake. Return is always an option if systems normalize but leaving may not be safe, or even possible after things get bad.

If you live near a major city you are not in much better shape. As food and water are exhausted in the city, desperate individuals and groups of desperate individuals will be spiraling out along major corridors in search of essentials. Predators will patrol major roads as they systematically loot homes for food, water and valuables. Living on the outskirts of a metropolitan area may be more dangerous because of a false sense of security. Reason to leave will not become apparent until any hope of safe travel is past. Do not over-estimate how secure a location is. If you live within twenty miles of an urban area or along a major highway, you are not in a good location. It would be wise to find a safe retreat and get there early.

If you live in the country, it is a better location as long as the home is at least twenty miles away from an urban area and fifty miles away from a large metropolitan area. The size of the nearest city matters. Large cities have established criminal elements already and they will become organized looters on the homes of the surrounding countryside. It is best to be well away from major highways as these will be natural paths for searchers fleeing the city as it becomes uninhabitable. A home that is fifty miles from a metropolitan city, the size of Dallas, TX, isn't very safe if it's just off the interstate highway, however another home that is only twenty miles from town may be more safe if travel over fifteen miles of county and unimproved roads is necessary to get there. Criminals are lazy and they will take paths of easiest picking. The most secure place would be in the country where trying to tell someone how to get there is next to impossible.

Having a retreat that is not continually inhabited, such as a deer lease cabin, is a good idea but be prepared to find armed squatters enjoying your provisions because no one was there to maintain a presence. There will be no police to call in a worst case scenario. It's a good plan, when maintaining a remote "safe house," to conceal provisions so they will not be easily found by others. Burying caches of supplies around the property will not only conceal them but will allow you access to them, even if the retreat home were taken. Large ice chests make good caches and with duct tape covering the seal, they will keep supplies safe and dry. Other good cache containers are five gallon food grade buckets with resealable lids. These can hold up to fifty pounds of food and supplies and are water tight. Please remember that during times of law and order, you are responsible for any harm that comes from the unintentional discovery and misuse of guns and ammunition that are not securely stored. When caching weapons or ammunition, it would be wise to store them in separate locations. Be sure to have a good map to locate the caches when needed.

Good, Better, Best

A preparedness plan may not be perfect but it should improve your situation. Those who live in the city are not in a good place and need a plan to get out. Moving to a place of refuge is imperative and it needs to be located and secured while things are still good. A vehicle that is rugged enough to drive to that place and enough fuel to get there without refueling is necessary. Six month's supply of provisions at that retreat location is a good start, twelve month's of provision is better. That plan moves you from a bad place to a **good** place. If you do not live near a metropolitan area but are near major highways, consider a plan to locate a **better** retreat in a more isolated area. If you can afford the lifestyle it would be **best** to live year round at an isolated retreat near a remote country town where there is a community already practicing the skills of independent living. No matter where you are in preparedness, your plan should be designed to improve your situation.

How Will We Know?

What might the signs be to indicate a genuine need to get to "higher ground?" For one, indicators will come quickly, even overnight. The morning news may report that America has defaulted on its National debt. That means our money has lost its backing and is worthless. There will be runs on the banks and grocery stores by those who did not prepare. When things like that happen, you will have about three or four days to get to where you need to be. After that, social disruption will start and travel will become dangerous. Disbelief will cloud the thinking of many as they wait too long to make their exodus from the city.

Terrorist attack may come violently or subtly (as in massive computer failures) but anything that causes the suspension of interstate trucking should be a definite signal to Get Out Of Dodge or stay put if you are already in a safe location.

Pandemics rise progressively and travel fast. There is a difference between a declared pandemic by the media and a real pandemic. Genuine pandemics leave hundreds to thousands of dead in their wake. If you hear of this in any major cities of the world and it begins to sweep America, it is time to make tracks to a retreat. Keep the phone open as long as possible and stay tuned to radio and TV coverage. I would rather side with caution and happily return home after an unexpected "remarkable recovery," than wait to travel after it became too late to assure my family's safety.

Like hurricanes, boarding up after the wind starts is not easy or safe and may not even be possible. Similarly, shopping for supplies and arranging a safe retreat location will be difficult if not impossible after crisis is upon us.

Natural Disasters almost always come quickly with little advance warning. They may make travel impossible but leaving ahead of a hurricane is good advice. If natural disaster hits your city, as an isolated incident, help will be on its way from other areas of our nation. If natural disaster affects large areas of our country, you may be on your own for a prolonged time.

GETTING OUT OF DODGE:

If your plan requires escape to a livable location, it is important to get going early. There will be three or four days of relative safety before social collapse begins. Map your route to avoid all major cities, because trouble begins there, and roads may already be blocked with others who are attempting to flee. Use county roads that avoid major cities by at least twenty miles. Carry enough fuel to make the complete trip because fuel will be practically unavailable twenty four hours after a major event. Travel in groups, when possible, and power drive to your destination by switching drivers. Time is of the essence.

11th HR

One Mogul at a Time

Just thinking of all these things can give you a headache; addressing each system to provide a reasonable backup, can turn that headache into a migraine. It can be a helpless feeling to realize where you need to be, how far you need to go and what is required to get there. Let me offer something I learned while snow skiing. In my youth I was at an intermediate skiing level and often attempted more difficult slopes than I was ready for. One such slope was at the end of a long traverse of flat trail. I should have had a clue to what was coming. Slope is a factor of distance traveled by amount of descent. Since the chairlift did the ascent for me, and I was traveling quite a while without much descent, ALL of the remaining descent was about to pile up fast. It did.

Tyler Woods

There I stood at the top of the largest and steepest slope of moguls I had ever seen. (For non-skiers, moguls are patterns of snow mounds usually created by the wind.) Worse was the line of people at the base of that hill, waiting to ride the chairlift. Those people looked like ants but I was certain they were all about to witness my making a total fool of myself as I tumbled down that hill. At least I had company. I was skiing with friends and one of the group had some very good advice for us. "Just keep your eyes on the next mogul."

That's what I did. Forgetting about where I needed to be and how far I had to go, I kept my focus on the next task at hand... how was I going to approach and handle the next mogul? There are many options with moguls just as there are with preparedness. You can turn before, on top of, or on the backside of moguls. With preparedness, you can address needs for food, fuel, first-aid or firearms. Just don't get bogged down with "where you need to be" and deal with what you can do right now. I made it down the hill with few mishaps and was surprised when I reached the base. I can imagine we also looked pretty good up there. No one watching could see our terrified hearts but they could see that we were tackling a huge task, one mogul at a time.

11th HR

Where to Start:

Begin a Community Group:

Of ultimate importance is the understanding that we need community. There are too many tasks and too many opportunities for failure to attempt a solo voyage through life without infrastructure. We all need sleep and that precludes our maintaining constant surveillance. Three families together would be better but a community of families is better still. The ideal would be that every family were prepared and banded together, however if that were possible, we would not be facing the situation at hand.

Prudence dictates that if the best answer to a failing infrastructure is a large community of like minded, prepared families, with skills and resources fit to assist each other in sustaining life. Anything we do to promote that community is a good thing.

Colloquium (CQ) Groups - by Brendon Hill in North Central Idaho

NOTE: The following section on CQ groups is provided by Brendon Hill and included with permission. Brendon has masterfully articulated how to develop strength into our communities through sharing knowledge. Brendon is available for personal preparation assistance:

Brendon Hill
Prepared Consulting Systems Inc.
brendon@preparedcs.com
www.preparedcs.com

The Beginning

CQ, to us, refers to our local community preparedness group that we started five months ago. CQ is actually short for Colloquium- which basically means an open discussion about various topics. I chose colloquium to shorten the even longer original name-"community preparedness meeting at the Big Cedar Schoolhouse" Whew! What a mouthful! You can see why it was abbreviated. I soon got tired of having to explain what a colloquium meant so CQ it became. I prefer the original and classical word but will concede to our generational ignorance caused by 100 years of government schooling.

The following is a concise record of how we formed our group, how it is organized, what it has accomplished and how it will continue to grow and mature. We are sharing this information in hope that you will be encouraged to take the same step and be empowered with information to be successful in your endeavors to organize your family, friends, neighborhood and community. So let us begin.

I gave careful consideration to individual prepping. Individual prepping leads quickly to recognition of the fact that you can't do everything yourself and the futility of trying. You need other people to complete the total package of fulfilling daily needs. No one person has the time, money or expertise to be a all-in-one survival community. Who would want to anyway? I like the idea of needing neighbors and sharing skills, assets and blessings. For instance, my wife is an excellent cook but I really enjoy potluck dinners. It gives you variety and flavor that you would otherwise never experience, especially desserts!

The CQ acorn was planted one sunny day when I was talking with two other 4H dads. The kids were busy with their 4H project so us Dad's started conversing about the bad state of affairs and the coming economic troubles. I then broached the subject and asked, "..wouldn't it be great if we all got together to discuss preparedness and get organized as a community?" The response was overwhelmingly positive. One of the men belonged to the LDS church and he gave me a thorough review of their church preparedness model and how they have a program dating back 60+ years. I was impressed. They have a great program and lots of resources for preparedness minded individuals. Just one problem. I'm not a member of the LDS church nor do I see myself joining their church.

I realized that I wanted to know more about their program but I didn't want to open the door for the "Amway Guy" either--if you get my drift. Once I started to inquire of acquaintances that were LDS I was pleasantly surprised that they actively encouraged all community members to prepare-whether they are LDS or not. They do so without proselytizing or recruiting. I haven't asked but I think they have a real common sense approach to preparedness philosophy. Every family outside their church who is prepared is one less community member who may need help when times get rough. They prepare for not just themselves but to dispense charity also. As for proselytizing, the young men on bikes will get to you eventually for a visit at your doorstep so let prepping be prepping and mission work be mission work.

I, obviously, can't speak for the LDS church but my dealings with them have been honest, straightforward and mutually respectful. I know they are LDS and they know I am a Christian Reformed Evangelical. So be it! We disagree on doctrinal issues but agree on the coming storm and we have grown to care for one another. Christ called us to be in the world and have dominion over our culture for Him. How can that happen if we don't have acquaintances outside the church-even friends who are of different faiths and beliefs? Being in the world is not being of the world-two different things. I retain close friendships for those who are of my covenant community all others are just friends or acquaintances. The point is don't be afraid to interact with the LDS or others. They won't bite.

Anyway, once I found out about their preparedness history and apparatus I asked how we could access those resources. I was encouraged to speak with people in the LDS church membership who had specific duties or leadership. In our area one individual had tried to start a community preparedness group but it only had buy-in from those who were LDS and no others. The problem was that non-LDS saw it as an LDS thing. I immediately realized the potential of garnering support from the vestiges of this group and build from there. One thing I hate is re-inventing the wheel and this would save us time and energy in getting the word out to potential attendees.

Each community has a business or businesses that have their pulse on the community. It may be a coffee shop or café where the locals meet and exchange information and discuss politics or the like. I was fortunate to find just the thing here in my small community. I explained to the man who owned the business my plan and he said it was a great idea and new for a fact that most of his customers would be interested. He also thought that CQ would succeed because I was organizing it. Meaning that would calm the fears of non-LDS folks and so we would see attendance from everyone. We also had another local asset, a small schoolhouse we could rent for $10 dollars. The location was central for all my neighbors as we are several miles out of town.

Choosing a good location is vital. An old-schoolhouse, grange, or community center. Making the location neutral is important as some folks don't like going into houses of worship not their own. Being considerate of the entire group can pave the way for much consensus and team building. Our location lasted two meeting before we moved it up the road to my own property. We have lasted two meetings here and now are moving it to a more public location due to growth and scope of CQ. Your location needs to have a few obvious and not so obvious essentials. The obvious are restrooms, water and power. I have learned the more amenities there are the more options you have for your topics. Cover from the elements, tables and even a dry erase board can add significantly your program. You may notice I didn't mention chairs as we have had our last two CQs outside and everyone brings there own lawn chair. By the time the weather turns we will be back indoors at a location that has all these things. Sound system is recommended once your group reaches 100 people otherwise its overkill for smaller groups.

Now that we knew we wanted a meeting and I had consensus of several community leaders (not politicians) we set a date and started formulating a game plan.

First rule--Focus on excellence and everything else will follow.
Focusing on excellence requires you to see through the small details that can aggravate and disrupt your groups momentum. Momentum or positive word-of-mouth reputation is important to get your neighbors involved. Once they've figured out they are missing something fun, innovative and worthwhile they will make an effort to attend.

Second Rule--Keep It Simple and Short.
All our CQ's are scheduled for Two hours every 1st Friday of the month. 6:30 pm to 8:30 pm with social time afterward so people can talk and network with each other. Our second CQ was so successful people stayed until 11:00 pm just to talk and network. We chose Friday nights for its ability to allow for later hours and it doesn't burn a weekend day which are a commodity in rural areas. We try to have four topics discussed in 20 minute segments. If a topic takes longer the presenter gets another slot the following month or gets a double. For example, our first and second CQ had a presentation on lighting in austere environments. The first CQ he covered oil or kerosene type lanterns. The next CQ he presented part two which covered pressure fuel (Coleman) lanterns. The CQ this last Friday we had a Physician's Assistant provide us a basic overview of the three styles of medical care: Grid Up, Wilderness, and Grid Down. This took 45 minutes

but set the foundation for future topics on medical issues moving forward. This has been our one exception to the 20 minute rule so each topic stays fresh and the attendees don't get lecture fatigue so changing topics every 20 minutes keeps fatigue to a minimum.

Third Rule--Focus on skill building.
Discernment of economic disasters and wisdom about our fragile society or thin veneer of civilized behavior is the foundation for a preparedness mindset. The building of skills becomes the obvious outcome of such knowledge. The skills that remove you from the J.I.T. supply chain are the skills we look to build in each other and ourselves. The following topics were covered in the last four CQs.

CQ-1: -Introduction to the concept and quick demographic survey.
-Pruning For Production-Fruit Trees and Bushes.
-Lighting: Lamps and Candles in Austere Environments.
-Beans, Bullets & Band-Aids-Various topics/open discussion.

CQ-2: -Review of Formal Emergency Management Plan for Area.
-Lighting: Lamps & Candles Cont.--Fuel Lanterns.
-Discussion of Topics for future CQ's.
-Beans, Bullets & Band-Aids-Various topics/open discussion.

CQ-3 -Review of Color Code of Awareness/Plan to design Color Code Emergency Action List.
-Latest CPR Techniques and Certification Signup.
-Radio Basics and Options.
-Water Production and Storage.
-Beans, Bullets & Band-Aids-Various topics/open discussion.

CQ-4 -Update on progress for Color Code Emergency Action List.
-General Advanced Medical Primer.
-Water Filtration, Purification and Storage.
-Knife and Blade Sharpening.

The topics were picked at random or by request. Again, keep it short and sweet. Those presenting topics should be experts in their field or have extensive knowledge otherwise you can see right through it. Focus on Excellence!

Fourth Rule--No Militia or Talk of Making War.
We all know the look. The look you get when you say "preparedness": like you've got three heads and just admitted you like country dancing with Bigfoot(for the record--Sasquatch don't dance, especially to country music!). If you want full community buy-in and support you have to be able to give guarantees that the war mongers among us are welcome but will not be given time to speak or recruit for there own self interest.

We do discuss guns, training and other topics pertaining to paramilitary preparedness but we declare up front that guns and gun training are for the gun range. There is a separate time and place that is appropriate for such discussion but CQ is not it. Paramilitary preparedness and training are subjects best discussed quietly amongst friends you know and trust--not publicly and especially not amongst a general populace. It will turn off a large percentage of attendees and kill any momentum you might be building. Again, focus on excellence by keeping topics short, concise and on schedule. **Do Not Give a Formal Platform to a Radical**. It will poison your efforts. I will discuss in Part Two how we handled just such an issue.

Fifth Rule--No Politics or Religion
CQ sees regular attendance by LDS members, Christians of different denominations and a family that are Messianic Jews. We are even seeing a growing contingency of granola folks. I hope "granola" is the right word to describe the holistic/organic living group without offense. I've slowly been educated by our neighbors who live this culture. I've learned they love to barbeque (non-meat dogs or turkey burgers), drink good beer (life's too short to drink bad beer) and some of them even love to shoot. Let's face reality--organic chips and salsa are the best!

What I'm trying to get at with rule number five is we need to focus on what we have in common--not what can divide us. Keep the group and discussion focused on skill building. One person described CQ as "4H on steroids" or "4H for adults". A perfect description.

Sixth Rule--Don't have a bunch of rules.
Over regulation, organization and rule making will turn people away. They want to come and be a part of something without having to join something. No call chains, emails or Yahoo groups. Again, keep it simple for you and them. You'll thank yourself later and they will thank you by attending and complimenting you on the quality and success of your meetings. An occasional pat on the back and slice of apple pie is all I need to do my part and it should be that simple for you also. If it isn't it's time to look in the mirror and ask why you want to lead such a group.

The first step in implementation is to find a few like-minded individuals with whom you can share ideas, receive counsel and help spread the word about the first CQ. As I mentioned previously I used the wisdom and connections of a local businessman who saw a lot of like-minded folks come through his door. I also sought counsel from a few others whose temperament and personalities were complementary to my own and conducive to a strong group bond. This core group was jokingly called "The Council" one day when my son asked who was coming over to sit by the fire for the evening.

I highly recommend anyone looking to start their own CQ, have something similar for guidance and input. Let me be very clear. Your council will fail you if it doesn't include your better half! I'm talking to you men! Your wives are there to complement and actually complete you. You are incomplete without her. Would you drive a car with only two good tires? Point: You won't get very far. They have insight, intuition and wisdom we don't. Include them from the start and it will go well with you.

Step two is to advertise your first CQ. Advertise quietly and by word of mouth only. Hand out fliers to just those friends and neighbors who might be interested. This will ensure a small turnout but a turnout with quality. Use the first CQ to work out the bugs. Have more discussion time and talk over your goals and plans. Take input and ideas and implement them into the next one. Once you are comfortable and see how it goes you can go bigger on the advertising by hanging up flyers.

Step Three is to make the CQ more sophisticated by offering more for attendees. For instance, we brought cookies and coffee/tea to the first two CQ's. The third CQ we started early and added a potluck meal fellowship time and then we added a campfire social to the end. Those wanting to hang out and talk did so until late into the evening. Ironically, we set up a big tent (borrowed from an attendee-keep it cheap) and the meeting ended up being held with 50 plus people standing around a large fire pit. Relaxed, cozy and warm. It felt like a big family gathering and was quite productive. All the subject content should be building upon previous CQ's. Say you start with basic seed sprouting, then small garden to large garden to greenhouse production. Simple to complex.

Step four is to add extracurricular activities as you and the group feel comfortable. For example, the first CQ we did a topic on Pruning. I offered a workshop the Saturday morning after the CQ and several people showed up to "watch" me prune fruit trees. It was very rewarding for them and after about ten minutes they went from pupils to management telling me which branches to cut and where. I finally had to chase them off by asking who wanted a turn.

At CQ-3 I sent a sign-up sheet around for a Utah conceal carry class. We had to have a minimum of 10 people to sign up to get the instructor to come to us saving us an hour travel time. We had nearly 20 signup. We are planning a mid-summer Barter Faire where no Federal Reserve Notes "money" can be used. Just barter with goods and services. All services need to be preparedness style goods. Breads, leather goods, knife sharpening, honey and other hand-made goods. No yard sale fodder allowed.

Also, we are planning several cider pressing days when the fruit comes in. I have also traded my jam making skills for access to acres of blackberries. We will pick and make jam the same day. I can taste the fruit of our labor already. Yum! These extra-curricular ideas can be timed to the season and community need like group firewood day or cider day.

Step Five is making sure you are ready for anti-CQ mentality. We experienced at CQ-2 a newcomer who was quite visibly agitated at the presenter who was reviewing a formal emergency management plan. Everyone in the room new this was a review of what the professionals use and was not intended for us as a group. The individual left agitated at the break. The next day I spoke with him and I thought I had clarified the direction of CQ enough for him to be satisfied. Boy was I wrong. The agitator then changed subjects.

He believed the CQ should be run differently and have a different focus. He seemed to have some valid points to his argument so I offered him the chance to present these ideas to the "Council". The mistake I made was offering empathy towards his ideas by stating some of them have merit. He took that to mean that I thought all his ideas had merit and that I just needed a little more information to make the changes he wanted-which wasn't the case. I think the meeting with the "Council" went quite well. This individual did convince us. He convinced us that there is a radical, self-serving segment to the survival community of wanna-be bad-asses who will do and say anything to create a fictitious resume of skills and expertise.

Let me be very clear. **Do Not Give Radicals a Formal Platform at your CQ.** They will instantly destroy your credibility and your groups momentum and attendance will suffer. We decided to graciously encourage this individual to go create his own militia or "Black Ops Group" as he called it. We let him know that we weren't as prepped as him and needed to focus on skill building or basically 4H for adults. Well, to say the least, this didn't work. He turned on the full court press trying to entice me to the dark side. The harder he pushed the more evident his lack of credibility became. I refused to respond and his final last gasp was an insulting email that included a personal threat to me. He even resorted to accusations of government conspiracy and infiltration by members of the "council" into our community. The final red flag for us was his incessant desire to be in control and make CQ into his own personal fantasy of *Red Dawn* in Idaho.

An interesting side note: A clear indication of embellishment of his expertise was the fact the he called himself an expert in preparedness but lacked basic knowledge of widely known preparedness resources.

Step Six is to embrace programs that already exist and can jumpstart your CQ or give it a definite boost. I don't like to re-invent the wheel so I looked to the local LDS community for what they already had rolling. We were able to join their local radio network making it even more community based and not LD- based. Once a month they do a radio check on GMRS radio frequency channel 20. The check is run professionally by the net command. They call out instructions in order of importance. Any emergency traffic is given immediate priority. Then a roll call of captains is taken. These captains are central to their area or neighborhood. The net commander then calls roll for each area/neighborhood and then visitors to the net get to call in.

The exercise is vital to where we live due to the mountainous terrain and lack of comms between valleys. Those on points and mountain tops complete the radio check by relaying to command messages and contact information. The last radio check on Sunday evening was impressive as to how far our net could reach and how professional all those taking part in it were. As we grow our CQ from the local to the regional this radio net will take on a whole new importance.

I've also learned that each LDS church has a local "purchasing agent" that actively pursues great bargains. All we had to do was ask to be put on her email list and we were in the loop on great purchases of long term storage food. When the email goes out you just reply to the instructions on where to pay and pick up the goods when they arrive.

We have also found out our county has a part time emergency management director. He has been a good source for print materials pertaining to disaster preparedness--specifically fire and pandemic. We hope to start working with him and the county on a county/regional plan through the political power CQ can wield as it grows.

Step Seven is to allow and encourage local businesses to participate. These local businesses can provide experts for your topic discussions and great locations to advertise your CQ and get people attending. One of our CQ topics was basic communications and radios. A local communications company attended and they gave a great lecture on radios and radio wave propagation with our local group in mind. They even brought examples of radios to buy and we discussed as a group what radio to standardize with for our communications net.

Another topic was water production and storage taught by a local well driller with 30 years experience in well and spring development. At our next CQ a local health food store will give a lecture on Home Herbal First Aid/Medical Kit-which will focus on grid down prevention.

These seven points are meant to help you implement and succeed with your own CQ.

1) Find like-minded individuals as your foundation.

2) Advertise quietly and purposefully.

3) Make subject content increasingly more sophisticated.

4) Added extra-curricular activities as you grow.

5) Be ready for antagonists.

6) Embrace other programs that already exist.

7) Encourage local business to participate.

All of these points are dependent upon your good listening skills, focus on excellence, and pursuing what can bring you and your community together rather than what can divide it.

Our CQ is organized along the following:

1) Individual Preparedness (**IP**)

2) Family or Group Preparedness (**F-GP**)

3) Community Preparedness (**CommP**)

4) Regional Preparedness (**RP**)

I've chosen to follow these four points when deciding what topics should be covered at CQ. These topics will generally focus on the first three pretty heavily and on the fourth lightly as I'm not inclined to create a bureaucracy. Some CQ's may actually have all topics focusing on IP but that may be by necessity due to the time of year, group dynamics or some other essential need or requirement.

IP is focusing on basic skill building. We do try to avoid topics that can encroach upon vocations that can create income during hard times. For instance, we have a group member who is actively perfecting her skills in soap making. We will avoid this topic in specifics but review in general terms as something someone can do for themselves. As a concession she has opted to help teach everyone how to make laundry soap that is far superior to store bought and costs under two cents per load. The idea is to cover general skills and let the individual decide on specialization for their own economic benefit.

F-GP is the natural byproduct of individual skill building. I consider this level the Beans, Bullets and Band-Aids option. This is were we present topics to help the correct, efficient and cost-saving acquisition of materials for families and groups. Our next CQ has two such topics-First Aid Kits and Home Herbal Medicine Kit. By covering these we are focusing on the materials that make up quality kits but will cover at another time the use thereof which would focus on the IP level. You could say this level focuses on the nuts and bolts of preparedness gear and supplies.

CommP we are beginning a two fold plan. The first part of the plan is to encourage growth of CQ groups in local communities in our county and adjacent counties. We started at the neighborhood level and have slowly accumulated members from neighboring areas and towns. We are now running ads in our local radio market advertising CQ for all the towns in the county. The ads are being paid for by one of our business partners who is also presenting a topic. This invite is basically for folks in our area to come and see for themselves and start networking to start their own CQ. Part two of this plan is an extracurricular part to CQ. This plan is designed to mitigate the effects of those in our local area who refuse or can't prepare for hard times.

As we all know there are individuals who will never see the wisdom of preparedness. There are also folks who haven't the means, wherewithal or character to prepare for leaner times. A comprehensive preparedness plan must take into account these people and how to deal with them. An immoral fantasy of large scale die-off or armed resolution is nonsense and evil. The possibility of large scale fatalities is real as well as the prospective use of force in defense of your property but to long for it or refuse to prepare to mitigate it is weak, lazy and unethical.

Our plan is to create a food acquisition, storage and distribution plan using the umbrella of an existing entity but run and managed by CQ members. The basic principle is to set up an apparatus that can submit for grant money, buy long-term storage food, secretly store the food and then distribute it safely in times of need. Now, please don't think this is a food bank approach. Let me explain further.

We have a community organization that is set up as a 501(c)(3) charitable organization. This group has paid the expense and taken the time to become a charity. There goal is to be an umbrella for the surrounding community organizations which allows them to apply for grant money using their IRS number. We are using this process for our local gun club to save time. The gun club registered with the state for $30 and now we can pursue grant money using the umbrella group. This food plan would pursue grant funds allowing us to buy a one year supply of long-term storage food for 500 people. Once food is purchased a secure location would be obtained for storage and an agreement with local churches to utilize their existing kitchens for distribution. Think of it as a level between individuals and the Red Cross. This would begin with one location and then branch out to other communities effectively covering all urban/small towns in our county.

We have received encouragement to proceed from the Sheriff's office and the county Emergency Management Director. They see it for what it is--an extra layer or buffer between chaos and order. The county likes the fact it's a private endeavor that requires no funding or oversight from them. It will or may require some security provisions when utilized but at that point security will involve the whole community under the sheriff's leadership anyway. This plan takes a little more time and effort but the rewards of having secure, private foods cache(s) for public distribution can relieve negative and immediate food concerns when troubled times hit.

RP is really just encouraging the first three in communities next to yours. We envision our CQ maturing in content and skills. While this occurs neighboring communities start CQs and do the same. We have two in the start-up phase right now. Once they mature they look to their borders to do the same. Think of it as a growing sphere of influence and protection. The greater the influence outward and away increases defense and potentially mitigates problems translocating to your area. We naturally or by other examples want some sort of leadership or formal organization. We can have the benefit of this without the headache or time-consuming investment. Let me explain.

Amateur Radio networks are the perfect apparatus to loosely organize the entire network in your area and eventually regionally and nationally. If our network here in Central Idaho matures and begins to grow outward we can add captains to each new area and eventually a group of ham captains to relay regionally and nationally. Again, I don't like to re-invent the wheel so I will look to established routes to achieve my goal. The last weekend of June is a National Radio Field Day for hams. They will spend 24 hours trying to reach as many contacts as possible. We will encourage those ham folks in our CQ to establish radio contacts outside our region such as Spokane, Boise, Missoula and farther away.

Likewise, new CQ groups with their local net will bump into each other as the CQ sphere of influence grows or as radio networks start overlapping. This model for expansion or connection reminds me of Subway sandwich shops and how they franchised in the early 1990s. You could find Subway's almost built on top of each other they way they expanded and allowed franchises to open. Let's hope CQ is so successful that it has the same "problem".

I'll leave you with one of my favorite quotes from the Holy Bible: *"The prudent see danger and take refuge, but the simple keep going and suffer for it."* - Proverbs 27:12.

Gloria Deo, - Brendon Hill, in North Central Idaho

Begin at Home:

Start a notebook to keep track of your resources, ideas and an outline to follow. Let me offer a simple outline that covers the major groups. I call it the Four F's. They are: FOOD, FUEL, FIRST AID and FIREARMS. There are other things to consider but these are the most important areas, in my understanding of preparedness during difficult times.

FOOD (& WATER):

Food and water are absolutely first on any list. The human body can survive thirty days without food but not much more than three days without water. Food and water will become a new currency. The recent earthquake in Haiti demonstrated this. Before the quake, people were poor and needy and would sell anything to you if you had money. Because Haiti is such a poor country, little money was required to appear rich by comparison. After the quake, perspective changed. A basket of money wouldn't buy much but a bottle of water would. The currency of the day had become food and water.

Take inventory of your home readiness as it stands right now. How long can you live without a trip to the grocery store? Is your family prepared? Most households average about ten days of food supply and many homes have far less.

Below is a link with some FEMA recommendations for home food storage.

http://www.aaoobfoods.com/amountstostore.htm

I recommend storing at least three months supply of canned, or dehydrated, 'ready to eat' food that requires little or no cooking. Cooking a pot of beans may seem like a good idea but the effect of the aroma of cooking food on large numbers of hungry people, may result in acts of desperation that you should seek to avoid. The first three months after the fall of infrastructure are the most difficult and is a time to maintain as low of a profile as possible. A good set of rules are, no lights, no travel and no smoke or cooking odors. Seek to be "invisible" in your environment. You are manning a lifeboat with your family inside. If you try to rescue more victims than you have resources to feed, the victims will still die but your family will go with them.

A new understanding of food will emerge. Since our caloric intake will need to double due to the physical nature of life after loss of infrastructure, the kinds of food we eat will also need to change. High calorie foods will be preferred to low fat or low calorie items. Potatoes, corn, carrots and peas will replace celery, lettuce and radishes. Breads will be heavier and perhaps made of whole wheat, corn or other grains. Since bread making will return to the home kitchen, the source of yeast may also change. Today we purchase packs of yeast from the grocery store. Tomorrow may require knowledge of how to culture leavening in the form of sour-dough or wild yeast. Baking powder might be replaced by buttermilk and soda. Food preparation may demand acquired skills that might be more easily learned before the internet and social groups become a thing of the past. Having a supply of wheat and grains does not assure the knowledge of how to convert that into bread for a family. As everyone knows, there is a lot more to cooking than buying the ingredients.

Finding wild food:

Never assume that because birds and animals eat something, that it is safe for humans. Their digestive system allows them to eat things that would certainly kill a normal person. There is a process to cautiously discover if a food source is safe but it takes some time and isn't something that should be attempted quickly. Never shortcut the procedure and follow each step in progression. If there is uncertainty of the results in any step, **STOP**. Let only one person conduct the testing.

LOOK: Attempt to identify the plant. Don't eat plants that are slimy, wilted or bug infested.

SMELL: Crush some of the perspective food and smell it for an odor similar to bitter almonds or peaches. If it smells anything like either of those two odors, discard the plant and DO NOT eat it as it may contain hydrocyanic acid which is a very deadly plant toxin.

SKIN TEST: Rub some of the crushed plant on tender skin such as the inside of the biceps. If there is any rash or irritation, wash it off and discard the plant.

LMT (Lips, Mouth, Tongue): Try putting a crushed portion of the plant on the lip, then in the corner of the mouth and finally on the tip of the tongue. Test these in sequence for twenty seconds each and if any location exhibits irritation, stop the test and discard the plant.

EAT SOME: If the plant passes all these tests, chew a small piece of the plant and swallow it. Do not eat or drink anything else for five hours. If there are no symptoms of sore throat, burning, nausea, belching or abdominal pain, the plant may be considered safe to eat.

Some additional cautions when evaluating plants for food are:

- Reject unknown plants with sticky, milky sap.
- Reject unknown red plants
- Reject plants with wilted or "old" leaves. Even blackberry, that is good to eat, becomes toxic when the leaves begin to wilt.
- Reject any seed or grain that is bitter or burns your mouth.
- Eat only fresh young plants.

Food Storage:

Food storage is easier than most would think. It takes some time, money and effort to gather, store, manage and rotate provisions but for the most part food supplies can be purchased at the grocery store. Warehouse grocery stores, such as Costco or Sam's Club and restaurant supply stores, are accustomed to large food purchases and no one will think twice about large acquisitions. However, large quantities of food can also be bought unnoticed at the local grocery store by simply shortening the time between shopping trips and purchasing a bit more than normal. It is not wise to advertise that you are storing food supplies. When the need arises, you don't want to be known as a resource.

Canned goods have a "freshness date" printed on the can and most advertise freshness for a couple of years. That date is a recommendation for freshness and full nutritional value. The Department of Agriculture tested canned goods that were over one hunderd years old and found them to be remarkably free of harmful bacteria with much of their nutritional value retained. I would not hesitate to eat canned goods that were several years old as long as the cans were in good physical condition and had maintained their vacuum seal. They may loose flavor and some nutrition but they will remain a food source long beyond the freshness date. Avoid cans that normally have a flat or concave lid, when the lid is domed. This indicates the growth of harmful bacteria.

Some products do not store well. Powdered milk is one of them. Milk is our primary source of calcium and vitamins A and D, besides being a key ingredient to many recipes. Regular powdered milk has a limited shelf life unless it is stored in an oxygen free environment, but there is good news. I've located a supplier of a milk alternative, made from whey (a milk by-product from making cheese,) that has all the calcium and vitamins A and D of regular milk and passes the taste test of many who don't like fat free powdered milk. It's good for cooking and stores five years or more. The cost is about $2/gal. Their weblink is: http://store.honeyvillegrain.com/driedmilkandeggs.aspx

[NOTE: I profit nothing by promoting this product. It's what I have purchased for my own family and I pass this on to you after a lot of personal investigation and price shopping.]

Flour and grain products are another problem. Whole grain is designed for long term storage. I'm told grain recovered from two thousand years of storage in an Egyptian pyramid had over a 50% germination rate. That means it retained its integrity and would also have remained a good food source. Flour, on the other hand, does not keep. As soon as the kernel and germ are crushed together, their "spoilage clock" starts ticking. Processed wheat flour loses nearly 80% of its nutritional value after only seventy-two hours and becomes rancid after about three months (depending on temperature.) Whole grain products should be stored in an oxygen free environment.

Food grade buckets are the containers that many restaurant and bakery food products are delivered in. They generally come with a lid that forms an air tight seal and are made of High Density Polyethylene (HDPE). As long as they did not hold food with strong odors, such as pickles, they are re-usable and convenient for storage of home food supplies. Should it become necessary to move to a safer location, five gallon buckets are the right size to quickly load fairly large quantities of supplies into a Bug-out vehicle.

HDPE

HDPE (high density polyethylene) is used in milk, juice and water containers in order to take advantage of its excellent protective barrier properties. Its chemical resistance properties also make it well suited for items such as containers for household chemicals and detergents. **Most five gallon food buckets are made from HDPE.**

Food grade five gallon buckets store nearly fifty pounds of wheat and have a re-closeable air tight seal. To make the container oxygen free, there are oxygen absorbing packets available through online survival stores, or dry ice may be used. To use dry ice, simply fill the bucket with grain and lay a hamburger size piece of dry ice, wrapped in a paper towel, on the wheat. Set the lid loosely on top of the bucket. After the dry ice "melts" the released carbon dioxide will have displaced the oxygen and the lid can be pressed onto the bucket. Mylar bucket liners are available from many online survival supply stores and offer an added level of protection. Another useful item for food storage is a vacuum sealer. These draw out air via vacuum and provide an air tight seal at the same time.

A good grain mill is an important tool of home preparedness. A grain mill will turn wheat into fine flour, corn into coarse cornmeal or a mixture of grains into a very coarse grind that will cook up to a great hot cereal.

When choosing a grain mill, it is important to consider the need for manual operation and the practicality of using an electric motor during times when electricity is available. As with most things, you only get what you pay for and a grain mill will be used to produce everything from flour for baking to cracked corn for chickens. It is expected to be capable of large quantity operation. I would steer away from cheaply made products that do better at filling my shelf than filling my needs. A good grain mill should last a lifetime with regular use and is worth the investment. One of the best mills is The Country Living Grain Mill. [I profit nothing by promoting these products.] The best price I've found is at: http://www.frugalsquirrels.com/store/index.html

Meat is a primary source of protein and poses a slight storage problem. Have you ever wondered how grandma kept meat when they didn't have electricity on the farm? The answer was canning. Almost any meat can be canned.

Canned food was a new concept in the early 19th century and Sir William Edward Parry brought canned provisions with him on two arctic expeditions to the Northwest Passage in the 1820's. A four pound can of roasted veal was recovered sometime later. The artifact was displayed in a museum until 1938 when it was opened and analyzed. The over one hundred year old contents were found to have retained most of its nutritional value and appeared to be in perfect condition. It was reportedly fed to a cat that seemed to enjoy it immensely with no following side effects.

Properly processed meat will last for years without refrigeration. Just short of a pound of lean ground beef will fit in a wide mouth pint jar and when it is removed it resembles a small meat loaf. A potato masher will break it into crumbles, ready for spaghetti or a favorite casserole. Stew meat is another good canning item and keeps its original juices for a quick soup or stew when added to a pot of dehydrated or canned vegetables. I have read the advantages of raw packed meat vs. seared or brazed & canned meat and have decided in favor of raw packed. The terms are misleading because either method results in a fully cooked product in a jar. "Raw packed" refers to the method of placing the food into the jars in raw form and then processing in a pressure canner for ninety minutes. After ninety minutes of pressure canning, no one has the option of ordering their steak rare and E-coli isn't going to happen as long as the seal remains intact on the jar.

[Editor's note – Thanks Pat!] Please take care when canning meat and vegetables. Follow the directions of a reliable source exactly. Ball Home Canning Products are the gold standard in home preserving supplies and their recipes are tried and true. Ball's Blue Book was a well-used book in our grandmother's kitchens and it, and more Ball recipe books, are still available. A clean kitchen and supplies are a must and your jars and lids must remain sterile.

Chicken cans well too. We have purchased whole chicken in a can, at the regular grocery store. It is very handy for making chicken soup in a hurry.

Tuna (any fish for that matter) will last for better than five years when canned. When we lived in the Pacific Northwest, we bought fresh tuna from commercial fishing boats at the docks. I found one quarter pint canning jars that looked like tuna cans made of glass. We canned our tuna and it turned out so well, we have never enjoyed commercial canned tuna since. I've also wondered how commercial brands can sell so much water in their cans of tuna. After squeezing out the water, there's not much tuna left.

Eggs can be had fresh by raising a few chickens. You don't have to become a chicken farmer to keep a family well supplied with eggs. Two or three chickens can produce a dozen eggs per week but they need a protected environment that is safe from predators. Please note that chickens don't produce eggs until they are six months old and they will take a vacation once a year to moult. Feed is reasonable when supplemented with stored whole grain that can be ground in a home grain mill. Chickens will find most of their food from the yard if they can "free range" and scratch for bugs. They need protection from predators, such as roaming dogs, that will try to pick up an easy lunch and eat tomorrow's breakfast before it's laid. Chickens also provide good barter material. A dozen fresh eggs will fetch high value when times are bad. Chicken manure is a rich source of fertilizer for the garden, after it's well composted. Many vegetables require large amounts of fertilizer to produce abundant fruit. Be sure to have a way of collecting and storing this valuable byproduct from the chickens.

Fresh produce from the garden is always welcome. Start gardening now because it takes time to work the soil and prepare a garden that produces well. Shop for "open pollinated" (OP) seed over "hybrid" seed. OP seed will produce fruit with seed that replicates itself. Seed collected from an OP variety of tomato will produce the same variety of tomato again. Hybrid seed is cross pollinated carefully to produce a specific result, usually a more commercially acceptable fruit with tougher skin so it won't bruise easily during shipment. When seed is collected from hybrid fruit the result may be a poor producing version of the parent plant or nothing at all. Many hybrid plants produce sterile seed. Since we are preparing for a worse case scenario, Wal-Mart may not be open for quite a while and some means of reproducing a garden without the spring seed sale is needed. By the way, Wal-Mart sells open pollinated seed next to their hybrid seed. OP seed does not need to be ordered from suppliers who triple the cost and then add excessive shipping and handling fees. Start learning how to grow plants from seed. I've had poor results from tasks I thought would be simple. Don't think you are prepared because you have a can of seed in your closet. Learn how to turn those seeds into something you can eat.

Select a site for the garden that can easily be watered by hand and easily watched over. Gardens are a target for night-time shoppers of all varieties. The garden needs to focus on high calorie foods such as potatoes, corn, carrots, peas and beans. Preferred foods will concentrate caloric intake and last through to the next harvest. Those who win this game will have become gardeners, hunters and fisherman.

Preserving garden produce is a popular job for a canner but a more practical and economical process for preserving vegetables is a food dryer. Dehydrated, or dried, produce takes far less space and does not use up as many canning jars and lids. Home dehydrators can be purchased or made with plans available on the internet. They are simple and effective. A friend of ours keeps her dehydrated vegetables in large jars in her kitchen. She can make a great vegetable beef stew in under an hour with a few handfuls of vegetables and a quart jar of canned stew meat. It tastes as if it was made from fresh ingredients and simmered all day.

Quantities:

Buying everything in one big shopping trip is probably not within your budget, now, or any time soon. Start by working toward gathering a three month supply of mostly canned and ready to eat foods that require only warming or the addition of hot water. Next, expand that to a six month supply to include dry foods and foods that require more conventional cooking. After that, push on toward a full year supply of food and necessities for those in your family. Finally, add as much as you can to help neighbors and friends who may not see the trouble coming. It's a long process but don't let the distance to the target get you down. Every step brings you closer.

Here again is the link to the FEMA recommendations for food quantity needs.

http://www.aaoobfoods.com/amountstostore.htm

Some quantities should come from data collected by those who have done the research and compiled needs based on a changing dynamic. The quantities recommended may seem high to a current lifestyle of 1500 calories per day but in the new dynamic of physical labor, your caloric needs will likely increase to 3000 calories per day.

Today, we buy our bread. When the system shuts down, we'll need to grind our flour and bake our bread. That requires some experience by those who already have the skills and know those quantities that we will need. However, it would be wise to become familiar with the art of bread making and the associated tasks of living "on the rough."

It will also be necessary to learn how to generate and maintain yeast for baking. Grandma did it and we can learn how.

A one hundred pound bag of popping corn isn't too much for a normal family. It can be ground to make corn meal or popped to make sweet or salty treats. When food quantities are managed, a bowl of popcorn will be very welcome.

A one year supply of wheat berries (whole wheat kernels before they are made into flour) is listed as seventy pounds per person. The same seventy pounds per person is recorded for white rice. Brown rice has more nutrition but doesn't keep as well. Salt should be stored in much larger quantities than dietary requirement because it will find use in meat preservation, baiting game and other creative uses. Unless access it available to clean ocean water for distillation of salt, it would be wise to store very large quantities of salt. Salt was one of the most sought after commodities by our pioneer ancestors.

Currently our family of three consumes a gallon of milk per week. That equates to fifty-two gallons per year or about ten cans of whey based milk substitute. Total cost for a one year supply of milk works out to about forty dollars per person. I would certainly store extra canned powdered milk as that would become a prized barter item during difficult times. It's cheap now but will grow in value faster than a stock market's wildest dream, when stores run out. Keep in mind that milk, bread and toilet paper are the first three things to vanish from store shelves, before a storm hits. Think of toilet paper as the new "white gold."

Vinegar should be stored at two gallons per person annually, for cooking, cleaning and canning.

Most regular food requirements can be determined by a current shopping list. How many cans of vegetables are purchased for the family on a weekly shopping trip? Multiply weekly needs by fifty-two after compensating for fresh vegetable purchases. If groceries are bought every two weeks, multiply the quantities by twenty six. It's not necessary to buy all the supply in one shopping trip. It is surprising how fast food accumulates by purchasing ten to twenty units of extra food each shopping trip and moving shopping trips a little closer together. This allows accumulation of storage needs without drawing attention to the supply. Remember, when a crisis comes, food and water may become the new currency. Public knowledge of a personal food supply could attract the wrong kind of attention.

When food is purchased for storage, think in terms of meals. When buying a canned ham, visualize how many meals that will make. For a family of three, a small canned ham will provide meat for one meal. That ham and its associated side dishes will be one third of a day's supply. Thinking in meals will help more than following a list made by someone else. Don't forget drinks such as tea and canned fruit juices. Bread and water may sustain life but variety makes it better. Stock spices too. Flavor means a lot and enjoyable meals will help during difficult times. Once you have your stockpile, begin rotating your supplies. Eat the oldest first and when replacements are purchased, put those to the back.

Keep cooking to a minimum for the first three months. Use ready to eat foods that need only warming. Better still are meals that fit the description of JAW food (Just Add Water.) Steaks on an outdoor grill will draw company from further down wind than one could guess. Much of the potential "company" that could be drawn to a home during these times, would not be welcome under any circumstance. Some would not think twice at making an armed visit after dark. Keep a low profile for the first three months.

Animals:

Please remember that long before the Purina company, there were dogs, cats and guinea pigs. Few died of starvation and most were fed scraps from the table, caught mice in the barn or ate grass and clover from the yard. Laying up a year's store of dog and cat food can take a lot of space and cost a lot of money. Plan on fixing a bit more for dinner and feeding the dog after the kids are full. In remote areas of Alaska and other places, dog owners make their own feed from corn or oatmeal mixed with ground fish or other meat sources. Do keep in mind that certain foods like onions and chocolate are not good for dogs. Dogs can provide warning of intruders and protection for livestock, but a well fed, yappy dog is also revealing of resources. If keeping a dog is planned, train it to keep quite unless there is a real problem. Our little dog would need a muzzle to keep quiet.

Livestock needs should be stored as well. Milk goats need good nutrition to produce well and though chickens seem to eat anything, they lay better with good feed.

Develop a regular practice of collecting and storing manure from livestock. Horses, cows, goats, rabbits and chickens all produce beneficial manure for the garden after it is well composted. Avoid fertilizing with manure from dogs, cats, humans or other omnivorous creatures as it can carry pathogens.

What I am about to say may appear harsh but the conditions in consideration are extreme. If faced with a decision between a family pet and a human family member's life, few would choose the pet. On the other hand, many are going to expend limited food and water resources trying to feed their pets and learn that, in the end, it cost them a human life. Failure to accurately assess your situation can be a deadly mistake.

Non Food Items:

Other necessary items are paper towels, paper plates, disposable eating utensils, paper cups, waterless hand sanitizer, water purification chemicals, TOILET PAPER (great barter material) shampoo, toiletries, feminine products, latex or nitrile gloves, rubbing alcohol and hydrogen peroxide. Just about anything used from the bathroom cabinet should be stocked. Kitchen items should be stored such as dish washing detergent, aluminum foil, plastic storage bags, manual can openers, an old fashioned camp fire coffee pot and large pots and pans. In a situation where several families join together to provide security and mutual assistance, larger groups of people will need to be fed. Plan on triple quantities.

What about water?

If the water pressure suddenly went to zero, do you have a means of getting water and making it safe to drink? We need about a gallon of water per day for each person. A six month supply of water for one person would weigh just under 1500 pounds. Storing that much bottled water would not be practical so a means of water treatment that assures removal of bio-toxins and pathogens is a must. Either a pump version water filter like those for back packing, or a gravity purifier like the Big Berkey, should be in the home. If there is no water other than municipal water systems, a plan to get to a safe place with a natural water source is appropriate.

If you are fortunate enough to have a good water well on your property, is there a means of getting that water to the surface after the power grid fails? Most well pumps require 220v and that requires a large generator that both consumes fuel and makes noise. That noise can be heard for miles when everything else is quiet and is a call to those who might be seeking victims with resources.

Hand pumps are not effective for deep wells unless one especially designed for that purpose. They cost hundreds of dollars. An alternative is called a "Bullet Bucket" or "Torpedo Bucket." They can be made or purchased. Price ranges from $40 to $90 but basically they are a tube with a flap valve at the bottom and a rope to pull it up from the well. The flap valve allows the bucket to fill from the bottom and when full, the weight of the water closes the valve.

I've designed a Torpedo Bucket that draws about a gallon of water, is easy to clean and maintain. It costs less than those I find for sale on the Internet. My teenage daughter can easily work it.

To use a Torpedo Bucket the well cap and well pump need to be pulled out of the well. Typically this involves loosening the bolts of the cap. Don't remove the bolts, just loosen them. The cap has a neoprene seal between the cap and a lower plate. The bolts sandwich this seal between the plates and when they are tightened, the seal expands to the well casing and provides an air tight closure.

Once the cap is removed, disconnect the electric line to the pump and the water line between the well and the house. It is assumed that the power has failed but turn off the breaker just in case power returns momentarily or from a neighbor's generator back-feeding the lines.

After the well is disconnected, some help is needed. Two men can normally pull a well pump if they are in reasonable shape. I've done it a few times. A younger third helper is handy for guiding the flexible water line, power cable and rope that runs from the well pump to the surface. My well is eighty-five feet deep and I pulled it by myself to change the pump once. I won't try that again if I don't have to.

After the pump is pulled, there should be no obstructions in the way. A Torpedo Bucket works great. Five gallons of water can be drawn in just a few minutes. Water drawn from a trusted good well should be purified after breaking the well's seal and pulling the pump. Contaminants have access to the water as soon as the seal is broken. Keep the opening to the well clean and covered when not in use.

Another method that doesn't require pulling the well pump is called an air lift pump. It uses rising air to draw and push water up and out of a well, much like a percolator in an old coffee pot. What is needed to build this pump is enough one inch PVC pipe to reach at least thirty to sixty feet below the water surface in the well. Attach a one-quarter inch, one hundred psi rated air hose to the outside of the PVC pipe. At the bottom end of the one inch PVC pipe, double the quarter inch hose back and into the end of the pipe. Secure the hose so that it will not come out of the open end of the pipe but do not block the pipe so that water cannot get past the hose. Lower the pipe with the hose into the well and fix it so that the end of the pipe cannot go further than sixty feet below the water level. Plumbers often use an oversized bicycle pump to pressure test lines to one hundred psi. Since forty-five psi is enough pressure to force air down to sixty feet, a pump like this works. When air is released into the open end of the one inch pipe, sixty feet below the water level, the rising air will create an expanding air dam that will lift water above it and draw water behind it. Multiple bursts of rising air lifts a large volume of water to the top of the one inch pipe, which can be directed into a cistern, bucket or barrel. Since the air is introduced into the pipe at three times atmospheric pressure, it will expand as it rises and accelerates water to the surface. Some find showers no longer necessary for the one collecting water, or some shielding might be advised to limit splashing of the "shotgun" water.

Water Purification:

With the absence of a sealed water system, consider any source of water as potentially contaminated. Contaminated water can make people very sick and without proper medical facilities, it could bring death. Fortunately, purifying water is not difficult. First, filter larger particles out of the water. Particles collect bacteria and make chlorination less effective. Filters designed for this are best but coffee filters or several layers of clothing can make a big difference in a pinch. If there are no other means of filtering the water, letting it sit undisturbed will settle most particles to the bottom of a container. After settling, draw the water from the top carefully. Filtered water should be brought to a rolling boil for at least one minute. Once cooled, add sixteen drops of regular unscented laundry bleach per gallon of water. Mix and let this stand for at least thirty minutes. After thirty minutes, if the smell of chlorine cannot be detected, add another sixteen drops of bleach, stir and smell it again after another thirty minutes. If the scent of chlorine is not present after the second treatment, discard the water and search for a new safe water source. Do not attempt to treat water that has a petroleum or chemical odor. For more information on emergency water purification, go to:

http://www.epa.gov/safewater/faq/emerg.html or
http://ldsprep.org/WATER.doc

Reverse Osmosis (R/O) systems, in many homes today, are good at purifying clear water but require pressure to operate and are very inefficient when it comes to the amount of water filtered vs. the amount of filtered water delivered. Most of the filtered water is dumped down the drain as bypass water. The bypass water can be collected and used for plant watering, laundry or toilet flushing. When there is an abundant supply of water, an R/O might provide a water purifying answer after a few requirements are met. FIRST – R/O units require water pressure between ten and twelve pounds to work. In a manual world, to develop ten pounds of water pressure from a water tower, the tank would need to be twenty-three feet above the R/O unit. Lifting five gallons of water twenty-three feet every day, would quickly get old. A better option would be a twelve volt "on-demand" RV water pump that can be purchased for about fifty dollars. Water would still need to be drawn to a ground level tank and electric power would need to be provided for the pump.

The internet has a lot of valuable information and I reference several good sites in this book but keep in mind that the internet will be down when the information is needed most. It would be wise to print critical information and store it in notebooks. If the resources are available now, laminate the pages in acid-free laminating sheets to protect them.

Finding Water:

A person can live thirty days without food but not much more than three days without water. Desperate people will kill for water yet it is fairly easy to find if you know where to look. Water sources can be found at the base of slopes in depressions where water naturally drains. If there are no streams or pools, look for patches of abnormally green or lush vegetation and dig there. If you come to a dried up stream bed or pond, try digging at the lowest point as the water may be just below the surface. An unusual patch of green vegetation on a hillside, may indicate the presence of a small spring of water coming to the surface. If you are traveling in mountain country, look for water trapped in rock depressions and crevices.

Suspect any pool that does not have vegetation growing around it or animal tracks to identify it as a watering hole. Check upstream for animal bones or carcasses that would pollute the water source. Look for the presence of green algae. Too much algae indicates the possible presence of fertilizer runoff and will make the water look like pea soup, no algae or dead algae may indicate pollution or the presence of toxins. Blue-green algae is poisonous. Check the edge of the source for mineral crust that might indicate alkaline water or pollutants.

Insects, especially bees, don't travel more than 4 miles from their water source or their hive. Flies rarely get more than one hundred yards from water and a column of ants heading straight up a tree are almost always going to a pocket of water trapped at the base of a branch.

Birds that feed on seed and grain, such as pigeons or finches, never travel far from their water sources. They also drink at dawn and dusk. These birds fly low and straight to their water but are heavier after drinking so they fly from tree to tree on the way back. Birds of prey seldom drink and birds that live on the water often travel great distances so they are not reliable indicators.

Animals will lead you to water also. Grazing animals are seldom far from their watering hole and drink at dusk and dawn. Follow converging game trails as they often lead to water. Carnivorous animals get hydration from the meat they eat and are not reliable indicators of water sources.

A **solar still** can be made by digging a hole and lining the bottom with green vegetation. Place a collecting cup in the center and cover the top of the hole with plastic. A small stone will weigh the plastic down in the center to make a drip cone. As the sun heats the cavity, moisture will condense on the plastic and drip down into the cup. It's a slow process but will provide at least some water. A solar still will draw moisture out of the ground and will distill clean water from ground soaked with urine, alkaline or salt water. NEVER drink any of these directly but after distillation, they all produce safe water to drink. Tieing cloth to your knees and calves and walking through vegetation will collect the morning dew. Once soaked, water can be sucked out of the cloth.

Snow and Ice can be melted for water. Select clean sources for either but keep in mind that ice will produce twice as much water for half the required heat when compared to snow. Please remember NOT to eat snow or ice for hydration. The calories required to melt snow or ice in your mouth would outweigh the benefits of what little water you would get. Exchanging core body temperature for a few grams of water is not a good trade.

11th HR

FUEL:

Everything runs on fuel of some sort. We have become so fuel dependent that we hardly think abut it anymore. Our ability to cook, drive, heat or cool, all depends on fuel of some kind. What would we do if we were completely cut off for an extended period? What kind of vehicle is best? How much fuel is enough? What are our fuel needs over six months? We will talk about transportation later but remember, driving will be almost excluded during an infrastructure shut-down so focus on cooking, heating, power generation and other necessary fuel requirements.

Fuel comes in various forms. Most is something to burn. Some keeps well but most has a limited shelf life. Gasoline runs many cars, power generators, and rototillers. It's convenient because we buy it at convenient service stations... until they close. What many don't realize is that gasoline has a storage life of only about three months. After that it either runs poorly or won't run an engine at all. Gasoline stabilizer extends the shelf life for about six months to a year. Gasoline is volatile and is not safe to store in large quantities. With as much gasoline as we consume in a week, I doubt we could store a year's supply without creating a serious hazard. Gasoline for storage should be purchased in the summer to avoid expansion problems from the butane added to winter gas (for better cold weather starts.) If you can purchase gasoline that does not contain alcohol (I've seen stations that advertised this) it will store longer. All gasoline for storage should be treated with stabilizer to prevent formation of gums that spoil the gas and it should be stored in air tight steel containers. Many plastic containers allow oxygen to permeate the sidewalls, spoiling the gas sooner.

A more stable and safe fuel to store is diesel. It keeps one to two years depending on type of storage container and temperature but much longer with diesel stabilizer. It can become fouled with algae and moisture but it is more stable than gasolene. Diesel's lower flash point makes it safer to store in larger quantities. Diesel generators are also quieter running and will attract less attention. Bio-diesel can also be made from used cooking oil some plants.

The champion of fuels is propane. Propane has no shelf life. A twenty year old tank of propane is as fresh as it was the day it was filled. The problem comes with converting a generator or garden roto-tiller to run on propane. It can be done but it takes some tinkering. Propane is perfect for heating things like the kitchen stove, water heater or outdoor grill. For a small investment a filling hose, to refill smaller tanks from larger ones, is available through propane distributors or from the internet. A used 240 gallon propane tank can be found for as little as one hundred-fifty dollars (craigslist) and will provide long term storage if it is in good condition. When assessing a perspective used tank, look for deep pitting from corrosion and see that the valves and gauges are in good working order.

Wood is a major heat source in colder climates where wood stoves are practical. Others use corn burning stoves where wood is not as plentiful but corn is. Some have a wood burning oven for cooking and as an alternative heat source. As always, exercise a lot of safety when working with open fire. Plans are available on the internet for outdoor wood fired bread ovens that can be made of stone, brick or adobe. They are fairly easy to build and work very well but must be constructed before the Hardware stores and supply centers close. *"Preparedness" stops when the crisis is at hand.*

Storing Fuel:

Keep in mind the 911 operator as well as the fire department personnel, will be at home addressing with their own needs and after the power grid fails the phones will most likely stop functioning. The thing to remember is that when crisis comes, **You're On Your Own (YOYO)** and there will be no police, fire and rescue. Safety is paramount. Keep fuels a safe distance from the home and plan for fire suppression with emergency shutoff valves, fire extinguishers, water buckets (filled at all times) and tools such as shovels and rakes. Our pioneer ancestors kept feed sacks handy to soak in water and use to beat out a fire. These sacks were sometimes fixed to a broom handle and kept in readiness to better reach hot flames.

Keep fuel stores out of sight. As with food and water, fuel will become a new currency. Keeping fuel tanks inside a shed or behind a fence is advisable but not close to the house. It is also wise to keep fuels separated to limit losses should one catch fire and take all fuel supplies together. Buried tanks are safest but only when they are rated for underground storage. A good rule is to never store fuel next to something more valuable than the fuel.

A Word about Generators:

Generators can provide conventional power for a time but consume great amounts of fuel and produce noise that can help predators.

After a December ice storm in the Pacific Northwest, my parent's home was without power for several days. After the second day I brought them a generator to refreeze their freezers and heat the house back up with the furnace. On bringing up the generator, it became vividly clear how noticeable the sound was to the neighbors. All the rest of the homes were dark so they knew by one look who had power. My Dad's phone rang, it was the neighbor down the street. "OK J__. We can hear the generator, but did you have to rub it in with the Christmas lights?" The call was in good fun and everyone's lights came back on two days later but the point is, when all is quiet, the sound of a running generator carries a long way.

Most domestic generators are only rated for infrequent use. Those rated for continuous duty are costly and still consume large fuel reserves. For long duration needs it is advised to consider solar cell technologies or other means that do not attract attention or consume fuel.

Batteries:

The war in Afghanistan could be lost for the want of batteries. Soldiers report the most critical supply items in their inventory are batteries. They power their communications, GPS, night vision goggles and a host of other mission critical equipment. There are a lot of battery powered items that we will greatly miss if there isn't a supply of batteries. Batteries come in several forms and plenty are needed. Alkaline batteries are known by the brand names Energizer and Duracell. These are good batteries but they are not rechargeable so once they are spent, there's nothing more to do than throw them away. Among the rechargeable batteries Nickle Metal Hydride (NiMH) holds a charge well and can be recharged many times without developing a memory. Battery memory is a condition that troubles Nickle Cadmium Batteries (NiCad.) When NiCad batteries are recharged several times before they have been completely depleted, the battery develops a condition where it shuts down completely when it is drained to the memory point, even though there is still charge left. Lithium Ion (Li-ion) batteries represent the best in available technology. They have long shelf life without losing charge, may be recharged repeatedly without developing memory and has great power to weight ratio. Lithium Ion batteries are the most popular choice for defense, automotive and aerospace electronics requiring battery power.

Wet cells are lead acid batteries and come in two basic styles depending on their intended use. Inside they have lead plates that are immersed in diluted sulfuric acid. Electricity is stored by means of a reversible chemical reaction. Wet cell batteries used in cars and trucks are designed for high current supply, for a short duration, to power the electric starter motor of an engine. To get that high current discharge (cranking power) the battery uses many thin lead plates. These plates can deliver high current for a short time but are too fragile to supply continuous power. They also cannot take the strain of charging a completely drained battery very often. To power lights, or other long term needs, a different kind of wet cell is required called a "deep cycle" battery. These batteries have thicker lead plates and can deliver less power for a longer time. They can repeatedly be completely drained of current and recharged without damage. The most common type of deep cycle battery is a golf cart battery. They supply six volts but two batteries connected in series, will deliver twelve volts. I used two of these for domestic power in our RV. We could run all the cabin lights for six hours each night and only required one charge every four or five days. Four or six of these would supply a lot of power for lighting and small fans and would make life a lot smoother after the loss of power. Golf Cart batteries can be purchased from Interstate Batteries, in "dry" form. Make sure to request them dry from the factory and not just emptied. "Dry" means they have never had electrolyte (acid) installed and these batteries will keep indefinitely until they are needed. Be sure to get the boxes of electrolyte with the batteries so they can be activated when needed. Also needed are rubber gloves, a rubber apron and a full face shield to properly fill and maintain the battery bank. Acid burns are more easily prevented than healed. The battery area needs to be well ventilated because lead-acid batteries emit hydrogen when they are charged and hydrogen is explosive when confined. With proper safety precautions, a battery bank isn't difficult to maintain and is safe. The safety precautions associated with batteries far outweigh those regarding lit candles and oil lamps.

With our supply of batteries comes the need to recharge them. I would recommend a solar array and a DC to DC charger. The most familiar battery chargers are AC to DC chargers but direct DC to DC chargers waste less power in the conversion process. Solar panels have a lower visible profile so they are not as easily noticed, unlike wind turbines. Solar panels can charge a battery bank to run an inverter for AC power as well as supply DC lighting after dark.

A note about lights; be sure to make good black-out curtains for any room intend to be illuminated. Uninvited guests will follow the 'welcome light' to any house that leaves a light for them to follow. Rolls of heavy black plastic and duct tape are good items to stock.

11th HR

First-Aid:

"First-Aid" includes all things medical. From daily vitamins to emergency surgery, both medical and dental. I don't propose that anyone become a heart surgeon via online education, but situations need a plan of action. Accidents are more likely with increased use of hand tools and injury is more likely in the shop than at a desk. Basic first aid and wound care are first on the list of acquired training.

A well stocked medical kit will contain a large supply of bandage items ranging from band-aids to large gauze pads and wound dressings. It should also include splint material, tapes, suture kits, antiseptic and antibiotic ointments, eye wash, tweezers, forceps, clamps and scissors (to list a few.) Plan enough supply to treat multiple incidents of many different injuries. Restocking the first-aid kit may not come soon.

Prescription Drugs:

For those on prescription medicine, speak to your doctor about getting at least ninety day supplies of necessary medications. The doctor may write a prescription for a six month supply but it will likely not be covered by medical plans since prescription insurance rarely covers more than a ninety day supply. Ordering medications from Canada may reduce the cost and their pharmacy controls put them on a par with US pharmacies. Mexico is another source as many antibiotics that would require a prescription in the States, are available Over The Counter (OTC) in Mexico.

When it comes to having drugs on hand to fight infection, I'm told livestock antibiotics, available in feed stores, will work just as well for humans. I'm not an authority but if I were fighting an infection without the help of professional doctors and clinics, I'd probably take my chances at becoming "healthy as a horse."

There are several basic antibiotics that are valuable to have on hand. Some fight respiratory infection while others work better for wounds. With some basic education you can learn which to use and how to use them. Advanced medical training is not required to learn how to properly use some basic medicine.

A good book to have on hand is:

Where There Is No Doctor: A Village Health Care Handbook (available at major book distributors)

OTC – Over The Counter Drugs:

OTC medications are powerful tools for keeping minor illness from becoming life threatening. Make sure medical supplies contain plenty of the following:

- Expectorants, antihistamines and decongestants to combat colds.

- Aspirin, Tylenol, Ibuprofen for fever and general muscle aches and pain.
- Imodium AD, gas X, Tums, stool softeners and laxatives for digestive disorders.

Treat any illness with caution during infrastructure failure. A cold can become pneumonia and constipation can become a potentially fatal impaction. Wounds are of particular concern. If a small scratch, becomes infected and goes untreated, it can turn the body "septic" with death as a result. Don't wait to see if a condition will get better on its own. Treat all abnormal conditions early. Change of diet and activity is certain to alter the digestion so make sure plenty of anti diarrhea as well as laxative medications are on hand, even if these are not used presently. It may take some time for digestive systems to adjust to new routines and foods.

There are some very useful multipurpose chemicals that could be helpful to the first aid kit and backpack survival kit. Potassium Permanganate ($KMnO_4$) is a purple powdered oxidant that is available in pool and chemical supply stores. It may also be found in some drug stores. When mixed with water to a pink color, the solution works to sterilize items. When mixed to a deeper pink it becomes an antiseptic. If it is mixed to concentrations that are fully red, it works well for treating fungal skin infections such as athlete's foot. Use caution and read all the precautions. $KmnO_4$ is a powerful oxidant that can ignite if mixed with other substances.

Natural Remedies:

Many natural cures have been replaced by items in our drugstore. So much so that we have forgotten how to use natural remedies. White wood ash, when mixed with water, will treat a sour stomach as well as any common antacid.

The woods are full of barks, herbs and plants that provided our ancestors with a medicine chest of cures, many of which gave birth to the products in our drugstores today. Books that help to identify and use these natural cures are available and will be of great value when the drugstores are no longer an option.

Training:

First-aid training is provided through the local Red-Cross, fire department or county agency. Cost is reasonable if not free. More advanced first-aid and first responder training is usually available at community colleges. Emergency responder and EMT training is sometimes offered at reduced cost when you join a local volunteer fire department. The important thing is to begin acquiring training for responding to situations that require intervention. Everything can't be learned at once but learning can start now. If all you do is start by buying an extra box of band-aids, at least it's a start. Just don't quit and call it good. Keep learning and keep moving toward preparedness.

11th HR

Firearms:

Civilization affords the luxury of not having to assume complete responsibility for everything. Meat comes from the market after the animals are raised, slaughtered, butchered and wrapped. Produce is farmed, harvested, transported and displayed for us. Fire departments stand ready to drive trucks, that cost more than our home, and put out our fires. Police patrol our neighborhoods to keep us safe from those who won't play by our rules.

For "thin spots" in our civilization, where these systems prove inadequate, we may raise our own food, install smoke detectors and fire extinguishers and employ security devices and personal firearms. If civilization as we know it, were to collapse, the full burden of its services falls upon the individual. Mike Arnold of Staying Alive, Inc. puts it this way: "The reason I carry a gun is because they are easier to carry than a policeman."

Preparedness is about self-reliance. Learning how to use the tools necessary for self-reliance is part of it. Firearms are a necessary tool to that end.

Firearms serve us in two major areas. They provide a means of taking game for food and they keep us from becoming victims by an outside threat. This is a serious issue and in the event of a major national crisis, where the infrastructure of society fails, protecting our property and life may demand a lethal response. I'm not sure who originally classified people into the three types: sheep, wolf and sheepdogs, but it's a good illustration. Sheep are the personality types that depend on others to protect them, feed them and care for all their needs. Wolves are the predators who victimize and feed on the sheep. Sheepdogs are the protectors who guard the sheep and slay the wolf. It is interesting to note that the sheep don't often appreciate the sheepdog until a wolf appears. For sheep, the thought of having a gun or using one for taking game or personal protection, may not be a nice thought... they need to get over it. Sheep end up as victims. A wolf is too busy searching for their next victim to worry about much. For the sheepdogs among us, this section comes easy because they already understand the need to get food and the need to protect themselves and the sheep under their care from the grade-A predators that will come.

Firearms for hunting:

NOTE: Gunshots are loud and can be heard for miles. Discharging a firearm should be an act of last resort during the first three months after the loss of infrastructure.

Archery and trapping are very effective means of hunting game. Our focus is on firearms because they serve the dual purposes of putting food on the table and facilitating personal defense.

Probably the most versatile weapon for hunting small game is the venerable 22 long rifle (22LR). It is very accurate and has a low report (not very loud) which allows the taking of small game without drawing as much attention as larger caliber guns. Ammunition is cheap and available almost anywhere ammunition is sold. There are many differing points of view concerning how much ammunition to stock but when it comes to low cost 22 long rifle cartridges, I'd keep at least 1000 rounds if not 2000. It will always be good barter when money fails. I would buy hollow point ammunition for its improved hunting performance.

My second personal favorite hunting gun is a 12 gauge pump shotgun. I favor 12 gauge because there are more choices of projectile ranging from light bird-shot for very small game, to buck-shot and solid slugs for deer size game. A 12 gauge shotgun with the right ammunition is a primary backup gun for bear hunting. It is a versatile and formidable weapon. For those buying their first 12 gauge shotgun, I would recommend NOT buying a "featherweight" (or light) model. Recoil is a factor of energy out the barrel against the mass of what launched it. A light shotgun can deliver punishing recoil. For some, a 12 gauge is too much gun and recoil is a problem. A close second choice would be a twenty gauge as they produce lighter recoil. Ammunition is more expensive and does not offer as wide of a range of options but it does still offer "bird-shot" to "buck-shot" and solid slugs for hunting deer. The range is not as good but it is adequate. Remember, it doesn't matter how fast or how often a target is missed. Only "hits" put meat on the table. It's difficult to hit the target when the shooter is worried about being hurt after the trigger is pulled.

Besides 22LR and shotgun, choices depend on what game is available to hunt in your area. Widely popular hunting rifles are 30-06, .308, 30-30 and .243. Each has its own strengths and there are many other choices of equally great calibers. My choices are made by how likely I am to find ammunition during difficult times. The more popular the caliber, the more likely it will be that I can find it. Keeping a large supply of hunting ammunition in popular calibers will also provide me good barter with those who didn't stock enough. Reloading reduces the price of purchasing commercially loaded ammunition.

You may notice that I have not listed a single handgun for hunting. Handguns have dropped every game animal in the continental US from grizzly bear to jack rabbit but they are still a handgun. They have shorter barrels and do not deliver the same energy or accuracy as that of a long gun. The purpose of a handgun is to keep a bad guy busy while you reach for your rifle. In a conflict between handgun and rifle, the rifle has clear advantage.

Firearms for Defense:

This is a truth of social disorder. Humanity is held together by social controls provided by our police, judicial system and National Guard. In the event of complete social collapse, our jails, prisons and state hospitals (including criminally insane) will be emptied to the streets. Looting will begin within the first week. The recent earthquakes in Haiti and Chile demonstrate how soon social decay begins. Poor government exacerbated the problem in Haiti, but in Chile the mean income of victims was much higher and looting became a serious problem after only six days. Pictures displayed well dressed people with arm loads of supplies taken from stores. For the most part, food and water were taken.

We have become a dependent society. Most American homes contain less than ten days food and in urban areas it is more like four or five days supply. In The History Channel's docu-drama, After Armageddon, a chilling comment was made that we are "nine meals away from anarchy." When social control is down and people get hungry, the thin shell of humanity cracks. Individual looting begins but is quickly replaced by collectives of ruthless and heavily armed gangs. Some of these will possess military-like organization and tactics that will make them a formidable adversary. As food and water are exhausted in the city, gangs of looters will set up ambush points to take supplies from travelers and conduct systematic house to house searches of homes near the city and along major roads. The only good option for those who live in urban areas is to get out early to a predetermined safe destination. That destination should be in a rural area and away from major roads. The reality of social collapse is that without our infrastructure of Police/Fire/Rescue, 911 operators, utility power and water systems, hospitals and food & fuel distribution, millions of people will die and there is nothing we can do to prevent it. Your home and food store is the lifeboat for the members of your family. Perhaps additional stores can be made for a select few others but accepting one more person than you have stores to feed could result in the loss of everyone that your lifeboat was designed to save.

A progression of social decay is following: This is a worse case scenario but there is a point where the loss of population can no longer support services as we know them. This could be caused by pandemic, war or biological terrorism but the end result remains the same. The massive armies of workers necessary to maintain our electric distribution grids, communication networks, petroleum refineries, fuel distribution networks and grocery retail markets could become too large of a demand on a reduced population. Without constant maintenance these systems fall into such disrepair that they would be difficult, if not impossible to restore. Currently, our country is able to restore small areas of damage due to storm or local natural disaster but restoration of services after significant national population loss would stagger the imagination.

The following is a natural progression of a complete collapse of our civilization. This is a worse case scenario and we all pray it never happens.

- Day one to day five: everything is pretty quiet after the news of the calamity. Most people stay home as neighbor's talk in an atmosphere of disbelief; waiting for the government to come to the rescue. Grocery stores emptied after the first day and fuel stations were sold out after the second day. All eyes and ears are tuned to continuing news coverage.
- Day six to ten: looting is starting and people are getting scared. Most are still waiting for the military or FEMA to arrive with food, water and civil order. Some will try to leave the city but will learn that the major roads are blocked by abandoned cars. Gridlocked traffic results

from accidents and cars that eventually ran out of fuel and formed an impasse.

- Sometime in the first few weeks: the power grid fails. Without constant maintenance, most grid distribution systems will suffer interruption within two weeks. Without power, sewers backup and city water systems begin to drain. TV and radio stations will go off-line. Looting will become more systematic and organized by well armed gangs.

- After two weeks: organized looters begin to spread outward from the cities which become uninhabitable. House to house raids for food, drugs and valuables sweep through outlying areas.

- After three months: millions will have died from illness, unavailable medical treatment, starvation and homicide. The volume of dead would exhaust the resources of our current system and with no organized process, decaying bodies of both animals and people will bring diseases, such as cholera, to claim even more lives. Cities will have become uninhabitable wastelands and life will be defined by a "new normal." Most looters will have died by this time, from lethal confrontations, gang wars, starvation and disease. Some will emerge to re-establish a social order.

Detroit Michigan is a sobering example of the result of economic failure. The cause of Detroit's troubles have been slowly coming but the end result appears to be the same. The city is dying and may never make a comeback. There is not enough tax revenue to maintain the systems necessary to keep things running.

Due to so much of the auto industry's outsourcing of manufacture to offshore countries, few meaningful jobs remain. The resulting drop in income and population (900,000 have left the city since 1950) has caused a steady decline in the average price of homes. In 2003 the average price of a home in Detroit was $98,000. By March of 2009, that average fell to $13,600 and today the average price of a home in

Detroit Michigan is $7000. If similar financial collapse were to affect the country at large and global conditions withheld assistance from our allies, America could quickly go the way of Detroit.

When presented with hunger and desperation, humans will progress through four normal stages to gain the things we need:

1) **Beg**: We will ask those we meet to share with us what they have in the hope that they take pity on us and share from their resource.

2) **Barter**: When begging fails we will trade what we have for what we need; from valuables to services, anything goes. Th is is a time when vital skills become truly valuable. A doctor or dentist may not have food or water but a community with food and water will share for his service. Gas welding and blacksmith skills, auto and small engine repair, tactical security services are but a few of the essential trades that will always be valued.

3) **Steal**: If we cannot reason with those we feel have what we need, we will resort to stealing what we believe we need to survive. "Scavenging" and "resourceful acquisition" are just other words for looting and stealing. What we would not consider under "normal" conditions will then become a new normal to stay alive. Earthquake victims in Haiti and Chile were not widely condemned when they looted stores for food and water during their time of need. They were driven by desperation to take extreme measures in order to stay alive.

4) **Kill**: When all else fails we will ultimately kill for what we need to survive. It would probably come first as a result of theft gone badly but in time, even killing will come easier as a survival tool. Trust will be out the window and every stranger suspected.

Four new principles will have to be accepted in a new world system following a complete collapse:

1) Life will not return to the old normal.

2) Many people, probably millions, are going to die and nothing can stop it. Pitiful people in desperate condition may have to be turned away because there isn't enough to share with them and continue living yourself.

3) Ruthless people will band together to survive by acts of atrocity.

4) It may become necessary to take human life to protect yourself and your family.

I have not mentioned anything about personal firearms yet. That's because the best way to practice self defense is to not have to use any. Prepare to not be there when trouble comes. In real gun battles, people get hurt on both sides and people die. Both sides lose. No matter how well you are protected, armed and organized, a lucky shot can find its mark. All said, tactical self defense is still necessary.

A tactical firearms course is highly recommended. Thankfully, God has designed us for peace and taking the life of another human being is something most of us are not ready to do. However, it is exactly what must be prepared for by those who intend to win this ultimate challenge. Those who cannot will become victims. When desperate times come, no stranger can be trusted and a plan for a potential lethal response to all contacts is wise. "Evil minded people" will masquerade as innocent lambs to get close enough to spring their trap. Without caution, you could become a victim.

Weapons for self defense are a last resort for situations that cannot be avoided. More about what is appropriate, for individual needs, comes with completion of a firearms training course, but here are some of my observations and recommendations. I am not going to explain all the 'jargon' of common firearms terminology. That is learned in firearms training. Purchasing a weapon without proper training may only provide additional weapons and ammunition for an assailant. Those with disciplined training become the winners.

Enough Gun:

Hand guns: Polar bears have been killed with 22LR bullets but I wouldn't bet my life on it. Enough mass and power are needed to quickly disable a threat. I personally favor a 45acp for its ability to quickly disable. The most common self defense caliber is arguably the 9mm due to increased firepower (capacity) and adequate power for most situations. Popularity and availability are growing for 40S&W making that another fair choice. In all, a well placed shot from a .380 will serve better than a miss from a cannon. Have at least 500 to 1000 rounds of ammunition for whatever handgun you decide upon. I would recommend against a revolver as a personal defense weapon. They have limited capacity of rounds (usually six) and are slower to reload. Under fire, not being able to reload quickly may mean that the good guy dies.

In social disorder, concealment is not required but would be wise. My personal pick would be:

- a medium frame semi-auto pistol,
- made by a reliable manufacturer,
- in a popular caliber (from 9mm to 45acp),
- that fits my hand,
- that I am comfortable shooting.

As for accuracy, keep in mind that the vast majority of incidents, where lethal force is warranted, occur within twenty feet with most of those occurring within ten feet. Only hits count, but those hits need to happen as quickly as they can. The most important point I need to make regarding accuracy is that you must practice. If your shot does not hit your intended target, it's going to hit something... or someone else.

Long guns: The purpose of a hand gun is to keep an assailant busy while you get to your long gun. Long guns for defense come in two types: shotguns and rifles. There is no more intimidating sight than the barrel of a twelve gauge shotgun pointed in your direction. Most police and military shotguns are twelve gauge pump action with improved cylinder bore and extended magazine tubes. My choice of loads is 2¾" number four buckshot. It carries twenty-seven pellets that are nearly one quarter inch diameter for a devastating effect. Works for me. The problem comes in carrying enough ammunition. Shotgun shells are bulky and heavy.

Mike Arnold of Staying Alive Inc. has a saying: "There are only two times when having too much ammo is a problem; when you fall into water or when you're on fire."

When it comes to tactical rifles there are two or three at the top of the list. The most widely sought after weapon system today is arguably the AR15. It isn't cheap but it does the job well and maintains practical accuracy and firepower out beyond 300 yards. The ammunition is light enough to carry a good quantity.

Another popular weapon system is the AK47. It offers a larger caliber and has the cost advantage and availability of cheap ammunition. The rifle is well built, very tolerant of dirty field conditions and ultimately reliable. The weak point is its effective range. Beyond 150 yards, the 7x39 cartridge loses steam and heads for the dirt fast. Most defensive encounters would be inside 100 yards and the AK47 or less expensive SKS offer adequate accuracy for home defense.

There are three requirements that determine the choice of a home defense long gun:

1) Firepower – high capacity is a must. High capacity magazines should be able to be swapped quickly. Both the AR15 and AK47 offer 30 round magazines.

2) Availability of ammunition. (Keeping 1000 rounds is adequate, twice that is not too much) If more peaceful times return, extra ammo will make great barter material.

3) Reliability – Both the AR15 and AK47 have acceptable field reliability.

Fancy scopes are not important for a home defense weapon. If a scope must be used, make sure it is a low power scope (1.5 to 3 power) to prevent tunnel vision that will limit seeing threats other than the initial target. Always have manual sights ready in case of optics failure.

Whatever weapon system is chosen, learn it inside and out and have a spare-parts kit to replace common wear parts. This should include extra bolts, extractors, firing pins and seals. A weapon is practicality worthless if it doesn't go bang when the trigger is pulled. Every person in the home should know how to use, clean and service every firearm available. In a family, everyone has to cover each others back. Even 8 and 10 year olds can learn how to take down, clean and repair an AR15 and their keen eyes will make them a better shot than many of us could hope to be. My teenage daughter is an excellent shot and can cover my back anytime. There's a reason the military likes the lightning reflexes and sharp eyesight of young soldiers.

Cleaning and Spare Parts:

Ownership requires learning how to care for firearms and keeping them in working order. "The loudest sound you will ever hear in a gunfight is CLICK." (Mike Arnold) A family could go hungry because a missed shot just scared the game away or you could lose your life because the one shot you had, never left the barrel. Keeping weapons clean and in good working order is a priority. This is one reason that I like the AR-15 weapon system. They are easy to field strip and clean. Standard field stripping and cleaning takes the weapon down to component parts for cleaning and examination for wear. Become familiar with every weapon in your arsenal. Be able to clean it, know the function of each piece and be able to replace common wear parts. There are spare-parts kits available for tactical rifles such as the AR-15 and one should be on hand for each weapon owned. You should have a good cleaning kit with ample supply of extra brushes, pads, solvents, cleaners and lubricants designed for weapon care. There won't be any sporting goods stores open when they are needed.

BEYOND THE FIRST FOUR:

The "Four F's" (Food, Fuel, First-aid and Firearms) are only a starting place. After the basics are covered, there are other things.

SANITATION:

In the absence of medical help sanitation becomes more than remembering to wash your hands before eating. Loss of refrigeration increases the possibility of food born pathogens, poor waste disposal attracts flies, improper sewage disposal can pollute your water source and dead bodies (animal or human) will breed and spread disease.

There will be no garbage collection so our disposal plan will have to change. Empty food containers should be evaluated for alternative use. They may not be making tin cans like they used to so wash and save any that could be usable. The same goes for plastic containers.

Containers that are discarded should be washed out or at least rinsed to reduce odors that attract flies and rodents.

Start a compost pile where non-meat food scraps (not fed to your animals) are composted. That compost can provide a rich soil for your garden but there is more to composting than making a pile of clippings and food scraps. Start learning how to manage a compost pile from websites devoted to this aspect of gardening. Composting requires temperature control and regular turning. If the pile is left to itself, internal oxygen levels will be exhausted and the temperature will not remain high enough to kill pathogens, weed seed, or the eggs of parasites, cysts and flies. Temperature monitoring and regular turning of the pile will keep temperatures high and the resulting compost safe.

For the reduced amount of actual garbage that will be created, bury it away from any well or water source. Remember that piles of garbage indicate to others that resources exist that they may want. Don't invite unwanted visitors and consider the garbage burial detail as a night activity for the first three months.

Stock ample supply of surface cleaner/disinfectant such as Lysol and Pine-sol. Cleanliness needs to become a passion and anything used to prepare, serve or eat food, should be cleaned and sanitized right away. Leftover food (even small amounts) will attract cockroaches, ants and pests of all kinds. The easiest way to deal with the problem is to maintain an ultra clean environment.

If your home appears safe and the plan is to stay put, make some preparations now that can be helpful during a crisis.

A gravity fed septic system and drain field requires no electricity and will continue to work until it is full, you can use water from washing clothes, dishes and bathing to fill the toilet tank for flushing. If the system needs electricity, other plans will have to be made. A well made pit toilet (outhouse) is not difficult to make but there are design requirements necessary to make them a more pleasant alternative to flush toilets.

How to Construct a Proper Out-House:

On a trip to Mexico, I was told by our missionary guide that we need to use the restroom at our motel prior to crossing into Mexico and to limit eating so that we would not need such facilities until our return. Being prior military, I was prepared for primitive plumbing and was very familiar with out-houses. Since I drank plenty of water due to the heat, I required a trip to the "shack out back." Upon locating said facilities, I found a shambles of boards just waiting to fall down, with a shower curtain door. These were "the facilities." No problem! All I needed was a discreet place to take care of business and I'd be on my way. When I stepped beyond the curtain, my life passed before my eyes, or was it my nose? The smell would have caused a buzzard to puke! For a people who are limited to this kind of plumbing, how did they not know how to construct a proper out-house? An out-house is more than a pit, a hole and a shack. Properly constructed, they are clean, sanitary and do not emit apocalyptic odor.

For the sake of those who may find themselves in need of constructing such a necessity, I've set to the task of building and documenting the finer techniques of out-house craftsmanship.

I built my "shack out back" on skids so the structure can be moved to new locations as the "pit" below, becomes adequately full. You can use two logs but pressure treated 4x6's work better if they are available.

My skids are about four feet apart with the cross pieces about three feet apart. I added another floor brace, half way between the cross pieces to support the floor and seat box.

Calking is applied to every piece as it goes together. Outhouse odor is caused by lighter than air vapors that offend our nose. The trick is to trap those vapors in the box that forms the seat and vent them outside the confines of "the library." The hole under the seat would normally allow those vapors an easy exit but the next photo shows another important part of good outhouse design.

An air-tight chute needs to be installed to deliver the "offending product" to the pit while blocking un-invited vapor from the library.

I used an old plastic five gallon bucket with the bottom cut off. These have a lip at the top so I cut the hole smaller than the lip and big enough for the bucket. With a little force, the bucket will fit tightly into the hole and after using plenty of caulking, I attached it to the decking with four galvanized sheet-rock screws. Any fasteners used in your outhouse should be galvanized or stainless steel due to the highly corrosive environment of outhouses.

The apron fits on the front and encloses the box. A regular toilet seat fits over the twelve inch opening of the five gallon bucket. Now comes the most important part. Trapping the vapors does little good if they don't have an easy way out. I used two inch PVC pipe for a chimney and sealed it to the seat box with caulk. You can use other sizes or other pipe. What is important is to give the rising vapors a way out from the seat box.

When digging the pit that the outhouse sits above, slant the bottom of the pit so that offending material won't pile up directly under the seat. You also should seal the outhouse over the pit by shoveling dirt against the skids and cross pieces. This will prevent wind from entering the pit and finding its way up the hole under the seat.

Until such time that your project needs to be functional, it can be put by the vegetable garden and used to store garden tools. It becomes a charming addition with purpose and few will realize that it's more than a garden shed "made to look like an outhouse."

Interment:

One of the most difficult aspects of the loss of our infrastructure will be death. Within a week, most families living in cities will be out of food. Pets will suffer first and those that cannot find food will die. Dead animals will not be picked up by Animal Control and their decaying remains will breed flies and disease if not buried in a timely manner. To a lesser degree, this will affect suburban and rural areas also. It doesn't matter whose pet or livestock has died, if the body is near your home the flies will respect no fence line. The only practical means of disposal for dead bodies is burial. Pets and livestock will not be the only bodies to deal with. There will be a lot of dead people too. Loss of medical support, heart attack, victims of assault and starvation will claim many. Morgues would be overwhelmed if they were open but there will be no such facilities available. This is just one reason why remaining in an urban environment is not survivable after the loss of infrastructure.

Another reality is that life may have to be taken in defense of your home and family. People driven by desperation will beg, barter, steal and kill to stay alive and that could be directed toward you and your family's resources. Taking a life may be the only defense. If that happens it would be best to record the circumstances and identity of the victim as best as can. Though it might be unpleasant, a digital photograph would be a good record. Should civilization return, an explanation for any grave sites on your property would be most appropriate.

CLOTHING & WASHING:

Our typical wardrobe today is unfit for expected conditions of extended outdoor physical activity, and exposure to the elements. The first rule of clothing needs to be, KEEP COVERED. Never walk barefoot, even in the house. Good foot care is important when even a minor foot injury can become a serious problem in the absence of medical attention. Good boots provide ankle support and need to be a priority along with clothes that protect from rain, wind and sun. I am not a fan of synthetic footwear. They may look good and they may be inexpensive to buy but after extended use, they fail. Runners pay eighty to one hundred dollars for a pair of road shoes that "go flat" after six to eight weeks of daily use. The shoe may look good but the synthetic cushion material collapses. Those who value their feet will get serious hiking boots from a reputable outfitter. Better made boots are leather and have stitched lug soles. They cost more but good boots won't be available after things shut down.

The backpacker's rule for clothing is "layers." You may have to pack what you can and bug out, so what you carry had better be good. Layering allows versatility with the addition or removal of layers to compensate for heat, cold or wet. Outer shells should be water resistant and loose fitting.

In cold weather, inner layers of fleece, wool or Orlon provide good thermal protection. These materials draw moisture away from the body and do not absorb them. Another rule of backpacker's is that "Cotton Kills." This is because cotton absorbs moisture and holds it next to the skin. More victims of exposure are found wearing cotton clothing than any other. It's difficult to stay warm when wet. Down feather sleeping bags are hardly sold for use in the lowlands. Down is a great insulator when it's dry but works about as well as wet newspaper if it isn't dry. Polar Gard®, Quallofil® and Hollofil 808® appear to rule the sleeping bag industry because they are very close to the insulation quality of down and will maintain that insulation even if it gets wet. Wool or synthetic socks and thermal underwear are important in cold weather. I am amazed at all the cotton thermal underwear sold in department stores. Cotton and cold weather are not a good combination. Buy synthetic, wool or Orlon thermal clothing.

In hot weather, a loose fitting water resistant outer shell is still needed. All clothing should be well fit but loose and non chaffing. Wear long sleeves and long pants. The best way to stay cool is to keep the sun off the skin. Camel riding Bedouins do not wear swimming suits, at least that we can see. Over the centuries, they have learned how to stay cool in the sun; they keep covered. That sun is not a friend and skin needs to be protected. With all the sun block sold, it would appear that we are a nation of nudists. No sun block made protects better than good clothing. Our family currently lives on the Gulf Coast of South Texas and my daughter spends a lot of time cooling off in the water. We bought her a "surf shirt" that has long sleeves, a high neck, and an SPF rating of forty-five. There is nothing attractive about looking like a lobster when young or having skin that looks like the backside of an elephant in middle age. When shopping for protective clothing at outfitter stores, such as REI, Bass Pro or Cabela's, they will often list the SPF (Sun Protection Factor) of their clothing. Some clothing blocks better than others.

For any weather, hats are back in. Our pioneer ancestors wore hats. They provide warmth in the cold, dry in the rain and cool in the heat. Fashion has lost its cover with the development of small cars and air conditioning. Another rule of the outdoors is "when your feet are cold, put on your hat." Nearly 30% of body heat is lost through our head. That is because so much blood goes to feed our brain. Hair is an insulator but not a good one. In cold weather wear a warm hat. When hot from hiking, take the hat off. Always keep a hat handy. In hot weather wear a broad brimmed hat that protects the ears and neck as well the face. When I first arrived in South Texas, I didn't wear a hat. A friend of mine told me "If you don't start wearing a good hat, the doctor will someday be taking your nose and ears off, one visit at a time." In our church we have had many members who spent long hours in the sun and are now paying for it with skin cancers. Some have come to church looking like a partially pealed potato after visiting their doctor for an annual checkup.

Sunglasses, hat and full cover are not just for sunny days either. The deception of cloud cover is that it blocks the sun. Clouds do block some of the sun but not the UV rays that cause sunburn and skin cancer. I have been sunburned worse on overcast days than clear days because I wasn't thinking about protective cover.

Protective clothing is important. Cuts, scrapes and injury should be avoided. Before performing tasks, think twice and wear protective clothing always. A scrape to a leather glove can't get infected but a scrape to a hand can. Protective eye-wear has stopped the need for more ER visits than any other item. Have them handy and use them.

Protective non-clothing

I've covered this in other areas but it's worth repeating. Store ample amounts of heavy black plastic for quick construction of everything from blackout curtains, shower enclosures and rain shelters. This stuff is the Duct Tape of construction material. Duct tape by the case, nails of all sizes, various sizes of "sheetrock screws", wire, rope, string and glue for repairing, creating and concealing, all of these will become vital assets when you find yourself on your own. Don't forget yards and yards of mosquito netting. When the county stops spraying for them, mosquitoes will become a health concern. Personal and residential bug repellant would be greatly appreciated but know how to properly use it and keep it away from sources of drinking water.

Laundry:

Keeping your clothing clean without electricity will be a challenge. There's always the option of a rock by the stream (if either are available) but it won't take long to wish for a better idea. Washboards are better decoration than a laundry tool and I'm sure they contributed to making laundries one of the earliest and most popular businesses in pioneer America. I am fascinated at the ingenuity of the Army Corps of Engineers who designed wind powered washing machines in Iwo Jima. They were not much more than a twenty-four inch fan driving a shaft that worked an agitator. A similar plan for making one can be seen at:

http://www.motherearthnews.com/Do-It-Yourself/1976-01-01/Cheap-Washing-Machines.aspx

All that is needed to wash clothes is a container to hold the wash, detergent and a means of agitating the clothes so the dirt can work its way out. A plastic tub and a toilet plunger will work. It only takes about two hundred plunges to wash a load and you don't have to work fast. Gentle agitation will do the job.

Ladies aprons may be back in style when washing returns to manual labor. Making an apron is easier than making the clothing it protects and they are easier to wash as well. Pioneer women bought simple dresses in dark colors and used various aprons to change the appearance. They could make a dress last for several days between washing because they kept it clean with aprons and full under clothing.

Since the invention of the electric and gas clothes dryer the clothesline has been all but forgotten. It will regain its place in the family when the electricity quits. Clothesline is still sold at the hardware store but it isn't available after stores close. Clothes pins will be in short supply and will become a prized item for barter as will canning lids and rings. A word of caution, clean clothes on a line is an advertisement of resources. It would be wise to dry your clothes out of sight (perhaps inside) for the first three months.

Bathing:

While vacationing in South Carolina, our family was introduced to the "outside shower." It had a dressing area and was completely private though "outside." With a little ingenuity an outside shower can be fashioned that uses an elevated water barrel (on the roof?) and some hose to reach the shower. Very little water pressure is needed and a hose left in the sun provides hot water all by itself.

Keeping clean helps to avoid illness so why not make it enjoyable. Anyone can take a bath out of a bucket.

FOOD PREPARATION:

The kitchen and food preparation utensils need to be very clean. Botulism grows easily and quickly in the absence of refrigeration. Washing down all surfaces with a bleach solution should become a regular practice. Be sure to let the solution stay in contact with work surfaces before it is dried off. Bleach needs time to work. You will want to stock up several gallons of regular unscented bleach to use for cleaning and water purification. Swimming pool "super shock" usually contains Calcium Hypochlorite and is little more than powdered bleach. When kept dry it has an effective shelf life of more than 10 years and one packet of Super Shock will make gallons of liquid bleach. Make sure to get Super Shock that does not contain copper or other algaecide.

Cooking presents some unique challenges without a stove or oven. Our pioneer ancestors were proficient at cooking meals over an open fire with cast iron. Cast iron cookware is still available and makes up most of what our family uses for stove-top cooking.

For outdoor baking there is a wonderful tool called a Dutch Oven. Camping versions of this 'pride of wagon train cookery' are available through *www.lodgemfg.com*. A camp version has a tight fitting flat lid that will hold hot coals on top while short feet on the bottom keep the oven over coals underneath. There are organizations and internet sites dedicated to the art of Dutch Oven cookery and they offer recipes and instruction. It would be a good art to learn while you can still call out for pizza if the first attempts don't turn out well.

A more conventional oven can be made from stone, brick or adobe. These were the bread ovens used in ancient times and continue today. Our family followed an interpretive trail that traced the work camps of men who carved highway 2 through the North Cascade Mountains of WA State. I was amazed at the 'piles of rock' that served as camp bread ovens. They were very simple but did the trick. The bread oven pictured is called a Horno and is the project of Jeff Ross. It's made of adobe and is one of the best I've seen. The principle of these basic ovens is to saturate the stone, brick or adobe with heat from a fire built inside the baking area. Once the oven is heated throughout, the coals are shoveled away and the bread is placed inside. Heat will "soak" out of the masonry and maintain sufficient temperature to bake bread, and other food, for several hours.

A "Rocket Stove" can be either purchased or made. These are very efficient, burn twigs, branches, pine cones or material that otherwise would be thrown away. Burning is almost smoke free after only minute or two of operation. You can learn more about these amazing stoves from an Internet search of "rocket stove." The best aspect of a Rocket Stove is the abundance of available fuel. An apple box of sticks can fuel a stove to cook a weeks worth of food for the family.

Fire:

My son and I made an overnight hike to a lake in the Cascade Mountains. We had packed a single burner camp stove and plenty of food. The weather forecast was for "a chance of a few showers" but we packed all our clothes in waterproof bags just the same. The trail was listed as "well maintained." We must have been lucky that day because it "chanced" all over us all the way to the lake. The "well maintained trail" turned out to be a dry creek bed that was about four to six inches short of being dry. By the time we got to the lake, we were drenched and it was getting dark. Our tent went up quickly and we tucked in for the night after a dinner of beef jerky and "Gorilla Cookies" (chocolate covered high energy bars). Morning found us well but hungry. The rain lasted all night but was light by breakfast. "Breakfast" it sounded so good and we could hardly wait to crank up the stove. To our dismay, a seal in the pump that pressurized the fuel tank, failed and we couldn't get the stove to burn. No problem, we gathered a pile of small sticks and dumped the white gas on them to start a fire. What a glorious fire we had.... for about a minute that is... then it died out, leaving us with a pile of steaming sticks and no more fuel. The next few hours proved to be a lesson we will never forget. Scrounging around that soaked forest for anything dry enough to burn was a challenge. I ended up splitting "wrist wood" (sticks about the diameter of your wrist) and carving out the dry wood slivers at the core. It wasn't easy to find dry wood because some was too green and others had begun to decompose and was damp. Once I had found enough wood that was dry inside, I had to carve out enough to build a fire hot enough to dry other sticks sufficiently to burn. It must have taken two hours to get a small fire burning, but by then my son's lips were beginning to turn blue. Our little fire was enough to heat about a pint of water in a canteen cup. We had fortified hot chocolate and oatmeal but were down to our last matches and using toilet paper for kindling.

The point of this is that fire making is necessary to keeping warm, dry and to cook food. If fire can't be made, it could cost a life. My son was inspired for his next 4-H project with a presentation that he titled, "A Spark Could Save Your Life." He got a blue ribbon for that speech.

Making fire doesn't have to be difficult if some preparations are made. We never go into the woods anymore without at least several backup plans for making fire.

Here are just a few of the easier ways to get some heat out of dry wood. Oh... that's the first thing, get some dry wood.

Fire also needs some tinder. Tinder can be dry grass or shredded cedar bark or wood shavings. Anything that will burn easily and can be fashioned into something like a bird's nest. Pre-build your fire with dry tinder covered loosely with small sticks and then larger sticks. Have a stack of dry wood available to feed your fire. You won't have time to go looking once the fire starts.

To start a fire a spark is needed. Sparks are tiny fires that can be built into bigger fires. Several different means are available to get a spark. A good one is called a match. Friction of the match on the striker causes the fuel at the tip of the match to ignite and burn the stick or cardboard as fuel. Simple.

Fine steel wool and a 9v battery will start a fire. Touch the battery to the fine steel wool and the steel wool will start glowing red hot almost instantly. You might want to have the fine steel wool already in your bird's nest of tinder before it's touched to the battery. As soon as the steel wool begins to glow, blow on it and gently fold it into the bird's nest of tinder. As the embers are enclosed with dry tinder, keep blowing on it and a lot of smoke should be coming out. Keep blowing and encouraging more smoke. In a few moments the tinder will come into flames. Place the burning tinder into the base of the pre-built stack of twigs and branches and a fire is on its way.

Char-cloth. Good tinder can be made ahead of time from squares of canvas (or old blue jeans) and a steel can with a tight fitting metal lid. Punch some nail-holes in the can, with the patches of canvas inside, and put the can into the coals of a hot fire. As the patches of cloth begin to char they will emit fumes that cannot burn for the lack of enough oxygen inside the can. Those fumes will flame as they exit the nail-holes. As soon as the flames stop around the nail-holes, your char-cloth is done. Fish out the can from the fire and let it cool. After it cools, open the can and retrieve the blackened cloth. Char-cloth keeps its shape but is fragile and easily broken so treat it gently. Char-cloth will ignite and glow with a very small spark.

Flint and steel is a material that when struck or scraped by a steel edge, will create sparks. They can be purchased in many camping departments from Wal-Mart to Cabela's. When the flint is struck, the scraped material sparks and falls onto the tinder, repeat the process of blowing and folding into the "bird's nest" as explained with the fine steel wool and battery method. I've started fire by flint and steel with dry grass as tinder but char-cloth works much faster.

Magnifying glass works when a fire is needed and the sun is shining but it is not reliable since a fire may be needed after dark.

Bow and spindle refers to a technique that once learned can be very effective and reliable. The best part is that nothing is required from the store. Select a resilient branch and cut it so that a 30" cord can be tied between both ends (this is the bow). The spindle is a straight piece of dry branch, about the thickness of your thumb and about the length of your hand from the longest finger to the beginning of the wrist. Round the ends so that one end is blunt and the other somewhat pointed. There are two more pieces to this device. A bobbin is a piece of wood that fits the palm of your hand and has a small round depression that will hold the more pointed end of the spindle. The bobbin keeps the spindle from wearing a hole in your hand. The last item is the baseboard. The baseboard is about the same thickness as the spindle. Measure in from the edge of the baseboard about the thickness of the spindle and carve out a depression half the diameter of the spindle so that the spindle can spin in it and be contained. Now wrap the string of the bow once around the middle of the spindle and trap the spindle between the bobbin in your hand and the depression in the baseboard. Pressing down with the bobbin and drawing the bow back and forth, make the spindle spin to burn out the hole in the board. A blackened hole should be visible with the edge about half the diameter of the spindle from the edge of the baseboard. Now cut a v-shaped notch from the edge of the board to just inside the edge of the burn hole. The notch should be wider on the bottom of the baseboard and narrower on the top. This notch is to catch burning embers from the friction of the spindle and the baseboard. Now place the notch hole over a flat piece of bark or thin piece of wood to catch the embers that will be made. Resume spinning the spindle in the hole while applying downward pressure with your free hand. Smoke should be very evident. Embers will begin collecting in the notch under the baseboard. Carefully lift the baseboard and gently blow on the pile of embers. Allow the pile to get hot and when it glows from gentle blowing, move it to the bird's nest of tinder and follow the process as with any other source of spark.

These are just a few of the ways to make fire. Become proficient at several methods by practicing them regularly. There is no substitute for experience.

COMMUNICATION:

My wife and I were attending a large meeting in downtown Seattle WA, when a tremor shook the building. I had my cell phone in hand and called home to see that our daughter was OK. She answered and all was fine, in less than thirty seconds I tried to call my parents who lived in Tacoma but my call would not go through. Less than thirty seconds after the tremor, all cell phone circuits were busy. I tried a pay phone and received a similar message regarding land line circuits. Telephone systems are not designed to handle uncharacteristically large volumes of calls. They are powered by battery and will stay up after commercial power fails but those battery systems typically only last a few days. In the event of serious infrastructure failure no phone systems will be reliable.

Television and radio also require power and employees to operate. In our scenario, they too will be down. The mail won't be delivered either.

Isolation is a powerful influence to bad ideas. POW's claim one of the worst aspects of imprisonment is the isolation. Not knowing what's going on or who's winning, not hearing from family or knowing if they are even alive will increase fears. Isolation is an enemy all by itself. Rumor will replace reliable news and wishful thinking will cause some to make dangerous travel to find their Shangri-La.

Various modes of communication offer different beneficial information. FRS and MURS radios provide walky-talky communication between members of your group. CB radio may offer some advanced warning of incoming groups of predators as well as local community news. The best source of information will come from shortwave radio. Trouble in America always seems to grab the spotlight in other countries. Having a shortwave radio receiver will at least provide important and reliable news.

Better would be to have long range two-way communication by means of a radio amateur license (HAM). Since 2007 the requirement for learning Morse Code has been dropped from the exam and acquiring the needed license has never been easier. With a few hundred watts of 12v power, communication with the world is possible. HAM radio amateur operators are helpful and willing to assist those in need. It will be difficult to find a better group to associate with.

LIGHTS:

Lighting is a luxury but can also be a hazard if it's from a flame. As romantic as candles and oil lamps are, they also have been the cause of many house fires. In a time when there are no 911 operators or fire departments to respond it isn't a good time to be playing with fire.

Fortunately, recent technology has created some interesting options. LED flashlights and lanterns are now efficient and attractive where older style incandescent lamps are a power drain. I replaced the lamp in my Mag-light with an LED and have yet to replace the batteries. LED lights emit a bright bluish-white light, they generate no perceivable heat and consume very little power. The lamps are rugged too.

Several lights with replacement parts and plenty of rechargeable batteries will offer a reliable source of lighting. A solar panel can charge batteries by day as they are used for lighting at night.

It is very important during the first three months to use blackout panels or curtains over all windows and doors in any rooms that will use lighting after dark. Make a trip around your home in the dark, while the lights are on, and look for evidence of light from around the windows. A small light will identify you as a target of opportunity to looters. Don't give them any help.

TRANSPORTATION:

Besides a packed and ready vehicle for emergency escape, I wouldn't plan to do any travel for at least the first three months. For the most part, those who prepared will be the only ones left alive after three months. There will be some who manage to acquire enough supply by less than honorable means but looting and roadside ambush will have greatly declined by then. I would still not trust strangers and always be wary of deception.

Gasoline will be precious as will diesel fuel. Small motorcycles will offer best fuel economy and bicycles will become popular again. Even with reduced hostility, I would not make any but the most essential travel plans. If travel can't be avoided, take enough fuel to make a round trip, including delays and detours. Bring several spare tires and extra water & oil. There will be no service stations and the roads will be trashed. Travel in pairs of vehicles if possible and have the trailing vehicle provide protective weapons cover as the lead vehicle passes through any Likely Ambush Points (LAP). After the lead vehicle passes the LAP, it can provide protective cover for the following vehicle to come through. This may sound overly cautious but narrow places in the road, underpasses and choke points in the road are extremely likely ambush points. The predators hide in cover until they see a potential victim but will stay in cover if they see a tactically challenging situation. Using tactical procedures through these points will hopefully assist in avoiding trouble.

Major thoroughfares are likely to be gridlocked by those who sought a better situation. Abandoned cars that ran out of fuel and the results of ambush are obstacles to travel. If travel is necessary, bring detailed paper maps to find back road alternates. GPS systems can't be trusted and will probably go down with the power grid. Be prepared for some back roads that are blocked by individuals or communities attempting to deter looters and refugees.

I recently purchased the best commercial truck road atlas that I could find and learned at its first use that it was great for the major highways but failed to provide detail when I needed back road alternatives. What I needed was a detailed county road map for every county along my route. A large collection of maps might be counter productive to mobility but maps that don't show the options needed are of little value. Collect county road maps for all likely and unlikely routes that might be taken. The less documented roads might turn out to be the better choices. Detailed area maps are often available for free from real estate offices.

HAND TOOLS:

Without power tools, we will have to learn again how to use hand tools. I would stock hammers, saws, planes, bit & brace as well as nails and screws of various size and type. Cutting firewood will require a good bow saw but a pruning saw will also be helpful. Bow saws and pruning saws cut through trees and branches much faster than saws designed for kiln dried lumber. A word of advice when using a hand saw, let the saw do the work. Adding downward force to a cutting stroke will cause the saw to bind up and get stuck. If firewood will be needed for winter heat, be sure to learn how to use a splitting maul, wedge & sledge and other tools for manual firewood processing. Chainsaws will be of little help with no fuel to run them. Stock plenty of rope, blue plastic tarps, plastic sheeting and duct tape by the case. Garden tools are available everywhere but good ones are hard to find. A really good garden hoe that is heavy enough to cut weeds and narrow enough to get into tight areas, will cost about thirty-five dollars. That's a far cry from the eight dollar garden hoe they sell at Wal-Mart. There is a big difference in tools. Tools that get the work done cost more but last longer. Cheap tools aren't worth the hole to bury them in. Don't forget a good round and square point shovel and digging tools such as picks and pry bars. A few "come-a-longs" and lengths of chain are useful. Just think about required tasks that must be performed and how they could be done without power tools.

Good quality tools are not much use if you don't know how to use them. Initiate small "hand tool only" building projects now and develop proficiency. It might surprise you how challenging it is to build some of the simplest projects when you are limited to all manual tools. You will be developing valuable skills for a post modern world.

TACTICAL ENHANCEMENTS:

"Defending your castle" will need to be a full time job. It is more than can be done by yourself and good reason to associate with several like minded families into a compound. A group of families can post twenty-four hour guard and man forward observation sites. If there is a large group of armed looters working your way, every bit of preparation time is to your advantage. FRS and MURS radios help with communication between members. Cell phones will be useless by that time. Night vision equipment is expensive but worth it's weight in food by the time the power fails. I read some good advice to purchase a removable night vision scope for your home defense tactical weapon. It will serve as a surveillance device and tactical scope.

Electronics fail but until they do, they can be useful. Driveway alert devices and motion detectors work when they are battery powered.

What can be done now is to create vantage points to keep watch over your property and remove natural blinds that might offer cover to the bad guys. Build "flower bed" mounds to present a barrier (natural cover) for your home. Our forefathers lived in substantial homes that would protect against wild animals and even bullets. Homes today are so soft, a bullet wouldn't be slowed much as it traveled through several walls. You can make ready by storing several hundred sand bags. They store flat and take up little room. When things get ugly, they will provide good defense for your home, after they are filled and stacked. You might stock a few extra rolls of barbed wire to enhance your fence line during the first few days of calamity.

[Another great editor note from Pat] Consider planting a "living fence" of thorny bushes like pyracantha (Common name is Fire Thorn. It also has edible berries); Acacia (Many of the Acacias have very sharp thorns, among the most useful is the Cat Claw. It has edible and medicinal uses); or Trifoliate Orange (Common name is Flying Dragon). Plant closely in double rows to make a very serious natural barrier.

11th HR

FAITH: the Fifth "F"

People of faith hold a precious resource for the desperate masses of a collapsed society. Faith will remain the only message of hope and deliverance for a world that is suffering under the weight of human failure. There will be many who blame God for the disasters, whether they be natural or otherwise. Some will claim that God is judging a particular sinful behavior, others will promote the idea that final judgment is at hand.

The Bible's order of end time events has the apocalyptic judgments occurring three and a half years after the rise of the great world leader. In the midst of severe adversity, people tend to ignore facts and jump to an emotional conclusion. Keep your Bible handy and read often.

Economic collapse, natural disaster, pandemic plague and enemy attack may be shocking to America but consider the rest of the world that faces these events regularly. Communist Russia saw revolution, purges, genocide and religious persecution for seventy-three years while America sat in freedom and prosperity. War has torn apart Southeast Asia and Africa for centuries. Guerrilla warfare and terrorism runs unbridled in Central America, Africa and Arab states. These calamities do not require a formal declaration of apocalypse to happen in America.

We can hardly blame God for the greed of our legislators and economic ruin of our country. We can also not blame Congress for the awful lack of statesmanship. They were elected by us and no other. It is our personal greed that elected representatives who promised to "bring home the bacon" for us. In one way or another, our collective votes are motivated by personal ambition over greater good; riches over righteousness and entitlement over opportunity. Collectively, our government IS the reflection of its people. If it fails, it will not be God's fault.

The same is true for any other calamity. God does not design diseases. They are the product of the genetic breakdown (for lack of a better term) of our civilization. Were it not for medical intervention, our life expectancy would likely be growing shorter than it is today but in the face of our great medical accomplishments, disease appears to be gaining on our ability to find drugs to fight them.

God's answer is regeneration through faith and ultimately a new body and new earth to live in.

Your faith is vital to that effort. *Romans 10:14* ought to be our marching orders; *"How then shall they call on him in whom they have not believed? And how shall they believe in him of whom they have not heard? And how shall they hear without a preacher?"* If we neglect the gift that is in us, what will the rest of mankind do?

Don't curse the darkness that is coming. God still cares for you. Remember, your light shines brightest in the darkness and we have the light.

11th HR

The Why of What We Do:

There is an awakening today to the need of making provision for times of adversity. The growth of internet survival supply and informational websites is staggering. While preparedness is a wise lifestyle for any time, it is easy to become so absorbed in the task that we lose our vision of "the why of what we do."

Just staying alive, with provisions to live out my days, is not a good reason for me to spend so much energy, time and expense in the doing of it. I need a purpose for my life. 'Just living' is not enough.

It is said that powerful unions brought about the demise of the railroads in America. The purpose of providing job security became paramount to the business of running a railroad. As radio and the telephone grew common, the need for telegraph operators became moot. Still, the railroad workers union demanded companies maintain these employees in their craft, at their same rate of pay, for as long as these workers chose to remain. A creative corporate manager gathered all his protected telegraph operators in a windowless warehouse where they were seated at telegraph stations that clearly had no wires connecting them to the outside world. They were each given a phone book and instructed to maintain their proficiency by keying the countless names and phone numbers. Though their jobs were secure as long as they came to work, all but one quit after three days and the last holdout didn't remain two weeks.

Survival by itself is not enough.

Do you know what lies ahead for the world according to the Bible? The events of our day fit powerfully in revealed scripture. Terrible times are ahead and the complete collapse of our government and infrastructure may only be a piece of the puzzle. There is a world leader coming who will be given power and authority, by most nations, without a shot fired or election held. What other reason could explain such a prediction unless the nations were in such a mess that no one else would want the job? America has become a police force for the world; but we, as a nation, are completely unplugged and off-line as far as scripture reveals. Most nations of the NATO alliance and European Union are listed under this new world leadership. America is not. We fade into the background and become insignificant to last day politics. An empowered America, as I know her, would not sit idly by as these things transpired among her allies.

The events that follow are not pretty. This unelected leader of the "new world" will assume great authority and make many new edicts for commerce and for "the better good" of all people. Resistance will not be tolerated. For three and one half years, healing will be evident and peace will prevail, then the bottom drops out. Apocalyptic catastrophes hit this world in waves. War, famine, disease, plague and destructive acts of nature, to name a few. Men will cry out to die rather than live under such conditions; then it gets worse. The world draws up sides for the greatest battle of all time. The aftermath of that battle will leave a pool of blood twenty-seven miles long and over three feet deep. No battle ever recorded will match this slaughter.

So tell me again, why would you wish to survive the coming near days of adversity so you could experience such holocaust? What is your purpose for deciding to live? The answer to this question will not only change your life practices but also your method and means of survival.

The only escape from this chaos is to recognize the root cause of suffering in the first place. Mankind has a propensity for violence and destructive behavior. Conquest at the expense of compassion is the law of our jungle. We were not created this way. Our condition is one of choice and the result of that choice was passed down the human bloodline so that now all mankind is affected. The end result is complete isolation from our creator unless something is done to fix it. The fix came by God's own hand through the blood sacrifice and resurrection of his son, Jesus Christ. The penalty for violation of God's standard of holiness is death. Jesus paid that debt and uttered from the cross, the greatest words we could ever hear: "It is finished!" The exercise of faith in Him as our only hope and Savior will alter our inner most being and create a new nature. It's called salvation. The blessings of that new relationship with our Creator include a soul cleansed of guilt, a real purpose in sharing the message of hope with people who desperately need it and at the end of our life, a new body and home forever without the limitations we currently face.

This message and our ability to share it with the lost souls in this life, is the only reason to live or stay alive on this planet that is headed for destruction.

The apostle Paul said, "For me to live is Christ, and to die is gain." *Philippians 1:21*

As we make preparation to feed and protect our loved ones, let's not fall into the trap of withdrawing to our castles and pulling up the drawbridge. If we are not about sharing the message of hope with a needy world, there's not much gain in staying alive.

I plan to defend my home and family with well planned "Operations Security" which will not exclude taking the lives of those who come to plunder by force. However, I will always keep a path open to help lost souls however I may. I'm making preparations for my family and as many neighbors as I can. Charity is a must if the message is to be heard.

Could it cost me my life? It can't, I've already received eternal life and to die would be my graduation. Until then, I'll live to serve and share so long as I can. Hopefully, there are many who still need to hear this.

11th HR

COMING OUT:

The first three months after the fall of infrastructure are the most dangerous. The worst of humanity will show itself and the best thing is to become invisible. Make no signs of life that would cause predators to look your way. This is why, for the first three months, I recommend canned foods that require little or no cooking and would create little food smells. The same goes for making smoke or setting a wash on the line or clearing ground for a garden. Those first three months are a life and death activity of hide and seek. Good planning gathers many like minded friends and prepared neighbors to join resources for watching each others backs. You will need twenty-four hour guards posted and good communication with other groups to gain advance notice of hostile activity.

After the first three months, most unprepared people, including predatory groups, will have died from starvation, violence or disease.

Cities will have become empty ghost towns but those who got out, and those who were prepared, will begin to mingle and circulate again. A new sense of community will emerge with small town government becoming the law of the land. There may even be a merging of resources as small communities form commune-like arrangements and share skills and services. There will continue to be areas of danger from surviving small armies that prey on communities for food in exchange for "protection." Those who refuse are attacked or killed by the very gangs offering protection. This is not just conjecture but has been played out in countries that have experienced infrastructure failure. These things happened in Bosnia and would happen anywhere for the same reasons.

Growing food will begin after the first three months. Everything will be worked by hand and emphasis will be on high calorie foods such as potatoes, corn, beets, carrots, peas and beans. With the increased physical labor, our daily calorie needs will grow to 3000 calories per day. Lettuce may be replaced by beets or turnips that provide green leafy tops and a bulky vegetable below.

People will again find time to worship and seek God. This is probably one of the few positive things to come of all the chaos.

Society will begin to rebuild. Order for a vastly different world will return.

SKILLS OF VALUE:

The cause for a loss of infrastructure will determine how soon and how much will return. In a collapse of our economic system, partial return may come within six months, provided we have assistance from otherwise healthy nations. This would most likely entail the re-structure of our country into four or five smaller independent states, much like the former Soviet Union which broke into nine Baltic states. Temporary currency to replace barter (called script) would begin after about six months with new international currency becoming accepted after five years or so.

If the failure were from a population loss, due to war, pandemic or extreme disaster, a complete return of infrastructure may not be possible. For example, power grids require armies of workers such as power plant operators, line workers, administration personnel and an array of support industry to maintain components like reactors, dams and turbines. If our remaining population were occupied with agriculture, without the use of farm machinery, we couldn't afford the manpower to restore the power grid. The same goes for the number of workers necessary to bring oil to the surface, transport it to refineries, convert it to various fuels and distribute it to retail stations from coast to coast. Without the oil industry, we can hardly support vehicular transportation, large scale manufacturing, or the myriad of systems that depend on fueled vehicles to perform their duties. Our systems are an interdependent house of cards and they may not be able to restart after their collapse.

There is a point where maintenance falls so far behind that restoration is impossible. A home is repairable if it has a roof leak but if that leak goes without repair, the ceiling will fall in, the floors will rot and the house will cave in on itself. Cities and the complex systems that they depend on, require constant maintenance to function. They cannot be "put into storage" for later use.

Determined by the level of social restoration, some skills could grow in value. Any form of manual mechanical repair will be needed. Gas welding will be available for a time but may be replaced by the skills of a blacksmith. Manufacture of pottery may graduate from hobby to a viable trade.

Gardening, hunting, fishing, sewing and bread baking could be universal home occupations. Methods of hunting and fishing will change. Attended fishing poles with a single hook and line will be replaced with trot lines, netting and fish traps. Traps will be checked daily as leisure fishing finds no time in our schedule of new tasks. Hunting will turn to traps and game seasons will be suspended in the absence of the Office of Game Management.

Hopefully, we will not see the complete removal of our support systems, but it is possible. Following a disruption, the lights could come back on, factories and refineries could return to operation and life as we know it could resume. It may take five years as it did for the people of the former Soviet Union and we may not be plunged back into pioneer existence.

Preparation, however, is having a backup for what "might" happen. Knowledge of how to live as a "new pioneer" may be the difference between who lives and who doesn't.

11th HR

THE NEXT STEP:

You have read my book, been acquainted with my experiences and advice, perhaps even attended one of my seminars... what will you do with all this?

Most thought this was going to be a light subject. Perhaps they assumed that after a week or two they could buy a few needed items and declare their family ready for whatever might come. My hope is that these realize that regaining self-reliance will be a major effort but is worth doing.

Three responses are open:

Option ONE:

Criticize the messenger, ridicule the statistics and go back to dependent life in a hope that it's all untrue. I sincerely hope it works out, and I mean that.

Option TWO:

Buy a few things off the shelf and then quit after realizing that real preparedness requires more change than was bargained for. Then settle back into the belief that what was done will be enough for something that "isn't going to happen anyway."

Option THREE:

Start a notebook and begin to change your life.

Self sufficiency enables you to be a messenger of hope for a world in chaos. You can begin subtly, helping your neighbors with words of encouragement and examples of kindness. Blessings from your garden, fresh eggs, fresh baked bread and a ready answer of the hope they see growing in you. We are not a people who should hide and become the stereotype of "Prepper Isolationist."

We need to understand that our awareness is not shared by all of those around us. How would you react if the first time you met someone, they blasted you with both barrels of "end of the world" disaster preparedness? You might offer to make them a tin-foil hat and a sign that says "Repent! The end is near!" Everyone is a light to their world. Let's choose to be an inviting candle in the window and not a detour warning. Our mission is to bring along as many as will listen and accept the free offer of God's grace.

I hope to see you on the other side.

Tyler